Contents

Acknowledgements

This monograph was coordinated by Prince Hussain Aga Khan, Farrokh Derakhshani, Nuha Ansari and Nadia Siméon on behalf of the steering committee of the 2007 Aga Khan Award for Architecture.

Texts were edited by Pamela Johnston with assistance from Rosa Ainley. Project descriptions are based on reports prepared by the 2007 on-site project reviewers.

Graphic Design: Irma Boom Office
(Irma Boom, Sonja Haller)

Published in 2007 by I.B. Tauris & Co Ltd
6 Salem Road, London W2 4BU
175 Fifth Avenue, New York NY 10010
www.ibtauris.com

In the United States of America and Canada distributed by Palgrave Macmillan, a division of St Martin's Press, 175 Fifth Avenue, New York NY 10010

© 2007 Aga Khan Award for Architecture

ISBN 978 1 84511 673 6

A full CIP record for this book is available from the British Library
A full CIP record is available from the Library of Congress

Library of Congress Catalog Card Number: available

Printed and bound in Singapore by KHL Printing Co Pte Ltd

Photo Credits

Selma al-Radi: 89-91; Amir Anoushfar: 57-65; Patrick Bingham-Hall: 73-75; Géraldine Bruneel: 25-27; Anne de Henning: 41-45, 48-49, 89-97; Farrokh Derakhshani: 139; Foster + Partners: 73, 75; GDP Architects: 73-81; Tim Griffith: 105, 109; Reha Günay: 89-91; Kurt Hörbst: 153-154; Hasan Huseyen: 137, 139, 141, 144-145; Birol K.S. Inan: 153-161; Jay, Studio Casagrande: 190-191; Hanif Kara: 74; Albert K.S. Lim: 105-113; Roger Moukarzel: 25-29, 32-33; K.L. Ng: 75; Nicosia Master Plan Team: 137-139, 143; Christian Richters: 121-129; Thomas Sagory: 41, 45-47; Laurent Séchaud: 57, 60; Solidere: 25, 27-31; UNDP: 138; Dimitris Vattis: 137-138, 140, 142; Nigel Young: 73-75, 79

Pages 182-187
Samir Abdulac, Kamran Adle, Mohammad Akram, Mokhless Al-Hariri-Rifa'i, Amir Anoushfar, Gregorius Antar, Chant Avedissian, Jacques Bétant, Timothy James Bradley, Cal-Earth Institute, Steven B. Cohn, Courtesy of ADAUA, Courtesy of Riyadh Development Authority, Murlidhar Dawani, Anne de Henning, Siméon Duchoud, Cemal Emden, Foster + Partners, German Archaeological, Murat Germen, A. Goldenberg, Reha Günay, Anwar Hossain, Hasan Huseyen, Birol K.S. Inan, Güven Inçirlioglu, Rohinton Irani, Barry Iverson, Jan Olav Jensen, Christian Lignon-Ransinangue, Albert K.S. Lim, Christopher Little, Pascal Maréchaux, Khedija M'Hadhebi, Kamel Nefzi, K.L. Ng, Gary Otte, Yatin Pandya, Mustafa Pehlivanoglu, Jacques Perez, Christian Richters, Serge Santelli, Hans Scholten, Onerva Utriainen

Drawings
All drawings are supplied by the architects, except those on pp. 84-85 and 87, which are from Jowa I. Kis-Jocak, and those on pp. 130, 133 and 135, which are from UNDP Cyprus.

INTER VENTION ARCHI TECTURE

Building for Change

I.B. Tauris & Co Ltd

Aga Khan Award for Architecture

Foreword

The role of most architectural awards is celebrating an architect's work or project at a given moment in history. The Aga Khan Award for Architecture goes beyond this, seeking to trigger debate and reflection on the built environment and play a positive part in improving it for generations to come. The award recognises work that addresses specific societal needs as well as wider contemporary concerns, and understands that successful projects are the outcome of a long and complex process of negotiation and collaboration between many different parties – between clients, planners, architects and craftsmen.

Every three years an independent master jury is confronted with between 300 and 500 projects that, taken together, represent the current state of the built environment in Muslim societies. The jury's first task is to shortlist a number of projects to be reviewed on site by technical experts. Six months later, the jury meets again to hear the findings of the reviewers and make a final selection of the projects that will share the prize money of US$500,000.

In this 10th award cycle a shortlist of 27 was narrowed down, during a week of deliberations, to a total of nine winning projects. As an aid to this process, the 2007 master jury drew up a series of keywords that marked the important issues they felt the projects should address: Collaboration, Education, Excellence, Sustainability, Sensitivity to Context, Negotiations, Changing the Status Quo, Interventions, Coherences, Transformations, Broader Context, Process, Architectural Ethnography, Affective Contribution, New Models of Urbanism, Accretive Urbanisation, Humane Urban Density, Dialogic *umma*, Contemporaneity, Translation and Transition.

These topics provided a basis for assessing the projects, though the list was continually added to as the specificities of each project raised further issues for consideration. Homi K. Bhabha's introductory essay elaborates on the jury's analytical tools, describing the thinking behind the selection process of the 10th award cycle. The introduction is followed by the master jury's official statement, detailed project descriptions and the jury's citations for all the winning projects.

The second section of the book encapsulates views and ideas that some members of the steering committee have been developing through this award cycle. Mohsen Mostafavi's article defines the notion of an ecological urbanism, Farshid Moussavi writes about cosmopolitanism and architecture, Omar Akbar speculates on the role of the city as a repository for collective memory, Modjtaba Sadria describes the multiple modernities that exist simultaneously in our complex world, and Billie Tsien looks at the effect that winning the award has had on the careers of younger architects. In addition, there are articles by members of the jury further elaborating their rationale in selecting the winning projects.

The last section of the book puts the award into context, offering an overview of 30 years of premiated projects as well as the award's other activities – the publications, presentations, seminars and events through which it has created opportunities for communicating architectural issues and sharing knowledge across the globe.

The world's largest prize for architecture, the Aga Khan Award for Architecture is a programme of the Aga Khan Trust for Culture, an organisation dedicated to revitalising culture and the built environment and improving the overall quality of life in societies where Muslims have a significant presence. The Aga Khan Trust for Culture is part of the Aga Khan Development Network, a family of institutions created by His Highness the Aga Khan with distinct yet complementary mandates to improve the welfare and prospects of people in countries in the developing world, particularly in Asia and Africa.

Farrokh Derakhshani

Architecture and Thought*

> It is all one to me whether or not a typical western scientist understands or appreciates my work, since he will not in any case understand the spirit in which I write. Our civilisation is characterised by the word 'progress'. Progress is its form rather than making it one of its features. Typically it constructs. It is occupied with building an ever more complicated structure. And even clarity is sought only as a means to this end, not as an end in itself. For me on the contrary clarity, perspecuity are valuable in themselves.
>
> I am not interested in constructing a building, as much as in having a perspicuous view of the foundations of possible buildings.

Ludwig Wittgenstein, *Culture and Value* (1930)

Ludwig Wittgenstein, the foremost linguistic philosopher of our time, built a house in Vienna in 1928 for his sister Gretl. As architecture, its success is controversial. Inspired by Adolf Loos's spare and static aesthetic, the design is intolerant of Art Deco embellishments or ingenious Bauhaus accoutrements. Wittgenstein himself considered it to be a 'hothouse plant': Gretl's house, he wrote, is 'an expression of great *understanding* (of a culture)… [but lacks] *primordial* life'.[1] Wittgenstein's other sister, Hermine, decided not to live in it because it felt more like a 'dwelling for the gods than for a small mortal like me.'[2] When I spent an evening there last year it was difficult to grasp the 'thought' of the house – Good architecture, Wittgenstein has suggested, expresses a *thought* – because the pristine spaces have been bowlderised by the Bulgarian government to fit its bureaucratic idea of a Cultural Centre. What remains of the original conception of this 'dwelling of the gods' is a strong sense that the spirit of architecture – the 'divinity' of any dwelling – lies in its human details.

Wittgenstein was obsessed by the clarity of the design as a whole and, in particular, by the way in which the details of the house – door knobs, windows, window-locks, screens, radiators – expressed its essential idea from different angles. But there is another sense in which these details of a house are human, even humane, components. A door knob immediately implies the hand that turns it and the eye that takes in the space that flows beyond the door; the window brings air into the house and breathes in the light; the screen is the skin that defines inside and outside, night and day, keeping them separate or allowing them to negotiate each other. The built environment is an ongoing, unfolding relationship between materials and humanity, between technology and psychology, between ethics and the environment. It is for this reason that architecture is amongst the most monumental of cultural constructions – functional, practical, durable, designed – and yet it only becomes Architecture when its presence is permeated with a 'thought' that overwhelms its physical presence. 'To try to make a building into architecture is a struggle',[3] Billie Tsien has written, as if to capture this very same idea: it is a struggle to find the aura that will not sanctify architecture but give it the spirit to survive. And it is to explore this idea of the value of architecture as *thought* – a concept at the heart of the Aga Khan Award – that I turn to Wittgenstein's scattered comments on architecture.

The jury may still be out on the architectural success of the Wittgenstein House. Nonetheless, Wittgenstein's writings frequently use architectural metaphors or analogies in order to 'model' conceptual problems, or questions of cultural value. For instance, in the passage I have quoted above, the concept of 'construction' is used to typify some aspects of a hegemonic 'western' ideology of history and social transformation shaped by the dominant values of Progress: an *uncritical* endorsement of modernisation (often identified with 'westernisation' or Eurocentrism); technological rationalism; triumphalist secularism; an unquestioned scientific world-view. 'Typically [Progress] constructs. It is occupied with building an ever more complicated structure.'[4] Wittgenstein opposes such a dominant narrative of Progress as much for its addiction to 'complication' as for its claim to be a sovereign cultural and historical 'value', subsuming all other qualities of life and thought – such as perspecuity and clarity – under its imperious sway. Progress, he argues in a democratic spirit, is one aspect of cultural value which should be equally weighted with others

6

such as Perspecuity: 'I am not interested in constructing a building, so much as in having a perspicuous view of the foundations of possible buildings.'

A relativist and relational sense of the pluralism of cultural values makes it possible to perceive the diverse social, ethical and philosophical 'grounds' (or foundations) on which systems of cultural and historical value are constructed *in relation to each other's differences and specificities*. Such a relational sense of cultural value – based on cultural difference and intercultural dialogue – is far better suited to a global ethic of inter-regional and transnational connections than to a normative, regulative idea of Progress that imposes a reign of homogeneity and hierarchy over other cultures and societies. And it is this ethic of global relatedness that reflects the ideals of a pluralist *umma* at the heart of Muslim societies which is repeatedly celebrated by the cycle of awards.

Wittgenstein thinks *through* architecture to give abstract thought a concrete quality that renders more visible its worldly implications and cultural values. The use of an 'architectural metaphor' for conceptual modelling bears a resemblance to the mobility of computer-generated graphics that display difficult dimensions and awkward angles that are inaccessible to the naked eye, and invisible to the linear logic of arguments. If good architecture expresses a thought, as Wittgenstein argues, then *good* thinking is enhanced by the use of the appropriate 'architectural metaphor'. *Good* thinking demands both clarity of intention and precision of purpose in the execution of a project – be it a building, a sculpture, or the drafting of a law; but such a project must be accompanied by a measure of ethical perspecuity that proposes a design for living – an architect's plan, an artist's vision, a politician's world-view – which aspires to some version of the good life, and contributes to a vision of the common good.

The close connection between good architecture and good 'thought' does not simply belong to the ivory-tower of philosophical speculation. The relationship between architectural vision and public virtue is a defining quality of the award's active engagement in endorsing the highest standards of professional expertise and technical innovation. This is as true of the construction of a modern urban complex, as it is of the restoration of a heritage site or the renovation of the infrastructure of an ancient city. What draws these diverse projects together from across the Muslim world – and allows a jury to act judiciously despite the eclectic nature of the nominations – is the dedication of the award to architectural values that embrace ethical and aesthetic criteria, in excess of the necessary provisions of professional 'good practice'. What are these architectural values? How does the architectural 'metaphor' enable us to model these values that belong to the world of 'building' or construction while participating in the *building* of the global world? What do I mean when I say that architectural 'thought' goes beyond the methods of professional practice?

Before I look ahead to the values – and metaphors – embodied in the 10th award cycle, let me answer these questions by looking back at the testimony of some of the jury members of the 9th award cycle. This glance at the past will provide some sense of the continuity of vision that accompanies the award. In the words of Reinhard Schulze, the constructed building is a mani-festation – a metaphoric expression, one might say – of a hidden meaning or a deeply embedded, invisible 'thought': 'To read architecture means to reconstruct the (hidden?) meaning that informed the building.'[5]

To reconstruct the hidden 'meaning' of a building is less like looking for a phrase in a language you know, than it is like interpreting an embedded genetic code. It is a process that combines continuities of form and tradition – a shared language – with surprising, even subversive, contingencies of historical fate and contextual 'meaning' that require us to revise our methods of judgement and interpretation. A great contribution to the built environment is made by architects, designers, engineers and builders, Babar Khan Mumtaz argues, but architectural 'thought' is more widely disseminated – it is a far more plural and diverse construction of social and symbolic value than the prerogatives of professionalism allow:

'[T]here are others who make a significant contribution to shaping, defining and developing architecture – and what is more, do so without building…This is more so if by architecture we mean not just a building or even a group of buildings by an architect or group of architects, but the output of a society, a culture or a period.'[6]

Good architecture develops through the evolution of the built environment, and by what is conveyed to architectural thought *without building*. 'We were architects, artists, philosophers and sociologists and we each took turns wearing the others' hats', Billie Tsien writes of her experience on the 9th award cycle jury. *Wearing the other's hat* ensures that the value-criteria of architectural success is relational and pluralist, and emerges out of an interdisciplinary dialogue of knowledges, practices and professions. On the process of judging, which always entails the weighing of values and the delicate adjustment of competing qualities, Tsien has this to say:

'The award carries with it the criterion of social responsibility, which is one that does not generally apply to architecture awards. I felt like a patient sitting in the chair of an optometrist's office. A large apparatus is lowered in front of my face…Which set is better – the first or the second? Which lens is the controlling one? There was a new lens set in front of my judgemental eyes. How do I see clearly with this new lens in place.'[7]

Wittgenstein's passion for a perpicuous view of the foundations of *possible* buildings is a way of creating a masterplan of the future that is open to new constructions of value, innovations in social utility, and developments in the creation of human community. Billie Tsien's desire to see clearly through a new lens results in a plea to 'try to make a building into architecture', which is a way of imbuing bricks and mortar with an idea, an aspiration, a 'thought' that exceeds successful construction and execution: 'It implies a belief in a shared future and a belief that the future can be made better. What better focus can there be for our lives here together on earth.' One of the central architectural values of the award is a profound sense of 'hopefulness' in the future, which is very different from a facile optimism based on paradigms of 'progress' that assume that history unfolds in a linear development. When progress is measured in this one-dimensional way, cultural values become polarised into 'clashes' of societies or civilisations, and the language of morality or mutuality is overtaken by the metaphors of war.

The ethic of hopefulness embodied by the award does not come a moment too soon in the dark days in which we live. If good architecture expresses thoughtfulness, in the positive sense, then recent times have provided us with tragic examples of the abuse of the ideals and icons of architecture. The brick-by-brick demolition of the Babri Masjid in Ayodhya at the hands of Hindu fundamentalists; the catastrophic crash into the Twin Towers in Manhattan by suicide bombers committed to *jihadist* beliefs; the barbaric gouging out of the Buddhas of Bamiyan from their timeless plinths of peace and contemplation: all these acts of violence and intolerance represent a kind of historical and aesthetic *hopelessness* that the award stands firmly against.

The cultural and social value of 'hopefulness', that I have attributed to the award, is intimately and instructively related to Wittgenstein's impatience with a monolithic notion of Progress. In serving to enhance architectural innovation in Muslim societies, the jurisdiction of the award includes Muslim nation-states, but goes beyond them to recognise Muslim societies as part of the global diaspora of peoples across the world. This has important territorial, temporal and cultural consequences. Ideologies of Progressivism are largely founded on the territorial concept of the nation-state; their historical narratives frequently oppose temporalities of traditionalism to modernity; pit the past against the present, and distinguish sharply between secularism and spirituality. Culturally, Progressivism attaches an inordinate importance to 'the present' as the pre-eminent value that gives cultural objects and practices their significance and relevance. The award is not simply *opposed* to the concept of Progress and its various coordinates. For instance, one could not

8

possibly dispute the historical sovereignty of the nation as the dominant political and territorial unit of modern society and the typical *form* of modern community; nor would one want to contest the importance of 'contemporaneity' as a critical measure of everyday life, or a temporal concept that shapes our historical reflections on the past and the future.

The award does not contest the validity of such concepts, nor does it set up a spurious contest between the east and the west, or between Muslim and non-Muslim societies. Such polarisations are quite out of keeping with the revisionary spirit of the award, which re-tools the terms and values of Progressivism to reflect the shifting and changing world of 'Muslim realities' that transform the global *umma*. A shift in vocabulary from Muslim *societies* to Muslim *realities* reflects the way we live today, as part of an intercultural, multi-faith world crossing cultural boundaries and national borders. We live in the midst of difficult transitions in custom and belief, and complicated translations of value and identity. *Transition* and *translation* are complex states of being that constitute the culture of everyday life in a global world. In a state of transition – or translation – you are caught *ambivalently* between identifying with an *establishing community* of 'origins' and 'traditions', while, *at the same time,* relating to an *empowering community* of revisionary values. 'Establishing' and 'Empowering' are only approximate, unfixed, terms of personal and social reference. I have named them thus, in order to reflect the commonly held view that, for instance, 'tradition' imparts a sense of the continuity of identity, while 'empowerment' is an invitation to experiment with newer self-identifications and emergent, experimental beliefs and collective values. This dynamic is as true of the diasporic condition as it is of transformations in the indigenous lives of those who stay at home.

This ambivalent condition of identification – and the 'double consciousness' that is its affective consequence – cannot be understood as a contest between orthodoxy and modernity, between faith and free-thinking, or the past and the present. No individual, group or society experiences social transition or cultural translation in neatly *polarised* parcels of contrasting views or contradictory values. This is because the coexistence of diverse cultural genealogies in national or transnational societies, or the prevalence of intergenerational conflict that reshapes cultural values, create life-worlds that are socially asymmetric, historically contingent, and morally puzzling. *How could highly trained Iraqi doctors or Indian computer engineers elect to follow religious customs so out of keeping with their 'western' professional training and their 'bourgeois' life-styles? Why would a second-generation migrant, born and educated in the 'liberal' British system, and working as an elementary school teacher, turn into a suicide bomber? Why does a thoroughly modern young European Muslim woman choose to wear a veil? Can democracy be established through the barrel of a foreign gun? Who pays the price of freedom when a whole society loses its life-world in the supposed act of 'emancipation'?*

However controversial these contemporary conundrums may be, they are unmistakably part of our post-9/11 global condition. The destruction of the Twin Towers was a terrifying, violent event enacted as much against a nation-state as against a particular architectural symbol and the values it represented as a material and metaphorical reality. In that sense, then, 9/11 was also an assault upon architectural 'thought' (whether or not one approved of the 'culture' of the World Trade Centre and what it stood for). However much you may agree or disagree with the 'content' of the questions I have posed above, each of them represents a 'double consciousness' and an ambivalent structure of identification that is becoming part of the popular, common knowledge of our times. You have heard these questions in conversation, in news broadcasts, on the lips of your friends and colleagues. They emerge from what I have proposed as the transitional/translation dynamic of contemporary culture where establishing communities and empowering communities are, at times, complementary to each other, and at other times in open conflict with each other.

Based on my experience of the discussions and debates of the master jury during the 10th award cycle, it is my view that the award's 'ethic of hopefulness' is based on a profound recognition of the uses and abuses of this important dynamic of global ambivalence. For ambivalence does not merely result in cultural confusion and conflict; it is not a state of moral ambiguity that leads to inaction or violence. To recognise the 'double consciousness' that exists in societies across the world is to acknowledge several important aspects of our contemporary predicament: that there is no neat division between east and west, now that we live in plural societies permeated with cultural differences; that the 'past' is not another country, as the phrase has it, because we experience the best and worst of the past in the very midst of what we value in the unfolding narrative of modernity, the history of 'our present'; that the engagement with the 'truths' of custom, faith and belief cannot be hived off from the 'knowledges' of the scientific world view because our affective lives demand forms of attention and contemplation that are not satisfied by the logic of 'reasons', 'causes' and 'claims.'

As award cycle follows award cycle, these intimations of 'hopefulness' come to be *translated* by the award into its institutional memory. This creates a tradition of architectural values that inspires its work at a very practical level. Architecture represents the most complex human negotiation between the need 'to belong' and be settled – to be *at home* – without having your worldly ambitions and affiliations constrained by retaining walls, village boundaries, city limits or national frontiers. There is more than a mere metaphor or image that connects the successful 'skin' of a building with the *affective, embodied* sense of satisfaction (or dissatisfaction) that it provides for its inhabitants.
It is this complex aspiration, with its uncertainties and necessities, that provided the range of *scale* that we had to consider as we worked through the nominations. For instance, the construction of a single school-house in rural Bangladesh, beautifully crafted from traditional, sustainable materials, provided both the serene *locality* of learning as well as the possibility for connecting and communicating with the world beyond. But the hand-made school-house had to be judged in relation to a a multi-million dollar Malaysian University, a transnational collaboration, that sought to create an innovative form of 'tropical architecture' suitable to local pedagogical conditions that also enhanced its global ambitions. By expanding the vocabulary of scale from problems of site, size and volume to encompass another meaning of 'scale' that signifies 'weighing scales' or the 'scales of judgement', we, as a jury, were able to negotiate the wide choice of projects before us, without losing the singular value of any one of them, large or small, simple or complex.

Perhaps the most intriguing and 'hopeful' issue that bounded our horizon as a jury was the scale and complexity of the *umma* itself. Many of our submissions occupied this problematic, yet productive, terrain somewhere in between our understanding of traditional Muslim societies and displaced and divergent Muslim realities. Change and challenging circumstances are, of course, part of both worlds; but the composition of contemporaneity, the speed of transformation, the conflict of values and the contingencies of 'identity' and solidarity that are part and parcel of the process of change may well be different. *The bridge between Muslim societies and Muslim realities is, at times, a bridge over troubled waters.* It was our privilege, as members of the master jury, to be faced with architectural projects that raised important issues about an *umma* that is democratic and dialogical, and maps both worlds, *not by sitting on the fence but by moving vigorously between worlds.* And this, again, requires a negotiation with cultural ambivalence. How should we evaluate a new housing scheme whose disposition of spaces harmoniously and homogeneously accommodates a community that is governed by strict rules of patriarchal power and authority? Does architectural excellence allow us to judge what may, or may not, be considered the 'good life' amongst different communities?

As a jury we were challenged to keep adjusting our critical and conceptual lenses as we moved across the varied landscapes of the *umma* and its architectural artefacts and practices: a market in small-town in Burkina Faso that becomes the model for a constellation of similar markets across the region; a school in Bangladesh that could be reproduced at low cost in other inaccessible, poor regions; sewerage systems in the dense urban conditions of ancient cities in Yemen; a small reflecting water-garden in Beirut located on an axis that gives the narrow site a deep, contemplative scale much larger than the ground on which it is built.

Scale is not merely a problem <u>internal</u> to architectural knowledge or practice; the scale of the contemporary *umma* reveals profound differences in sites and localities – rural communities, small towns, industrial cities, private homes, public institutions – that demand design-imagination and material, practical interventions. Scale is, indeed, an architectural *intervention* that both responds to site-specificity while, at the same time, *creating* or constructing a sense of *locality* (which is never simply a given, a priori reality). In that sense, scale is also an issue of the ethics of architecture – what one chooses to build, who one chooses to build *for*, and the values that the building represents in-itself and in relation to others.

A different kind of lens snapped into place when we took up questions of conservation and restoration – which are after all, issues of the 'time-scale' of the built environment. Conservation and restoration are often thought of as processes of 'pickling' the past in the present, and fetishising the aura of antiquity. But if you approach these issues from the perspective of cultural translation – premised on the *ongoing* presence of the past-in-the present rather than the polarity of tradition vs modernity – then conservation and restoration become our commitments to keeping alive the 'hopefulness' of history. Conservation/restoration is not about asserting the permanence of the past, but its productive contribution to the future. Restoration is a work in progress, but so is human history, and the narrative of each individual life. The *revisionary* emphasis of restoration/ conservation shares a dynamic relation to the past which is visible in contemporary projects. For instance, two young Singaporean architects recreate the traditional 'monsoon-window' for a modern apartment building that consequently becomes less dependent upon air-conditioning and lightens the load on an overburdened electricity grid.

'Scale' – in the anti-progressivist mode – represents an architectural and ethical commitment to what Wittgenstein describes as *not* 'constructing a building, as much as in having a perspicuous view of the foundations of possible buildings.' Conservation/restoration, I have argued, are not about the past but imbue architectural values with a 'thought' of the future. In this sequence of architectural 'hopefulness' there is no responsibility to the environment as important as the commitment to sustainability. Sustainability, as a scale of judgement, creates an architecture that is only partially about 'building'. As the best of our nominations readily persuaded us, sustainability is about creating environments committed to survival and well-being – to shared expressions of neighbourhood and solidarity that are intolerant of assumptions of cultural supremacy.

'Remember the impression one gets from good architecture, that it expresses a thought', Wittgenstein writes. 'It makes one want to respond with a gesture.'[8] A gesture, for Wittgenstein, is something that is insinuated into life, becomes an infinitely varied process of interpretation and response, and encourages dialogue. In the fullest sense of the word, the award is a 'gesture' that responds to architecture, not only as construction and building but also as a contribution to the best that is 'thought' in the world of architectural values.

Homi K. Bhabha

* For my dear friend Anish Kapoor, to thank him for his indulgence and inspiration.

1. Wittgenstein, *Culture and Value*, Chicago, 7e, 38.
2. 'A Dwelling for the Gods', by Stuart Jeffries, *Guardian*, 5 January 2002.
3. *Architecture and Polyphony*, London, 143.
4. *Culture and Value*.
5. *Architecture and Polyphony*, 140.
6. ibid. 151.
7. ibid. 143.
8. *Culture and Value*, 22e.

Statement of the Master Jury

The 2007 Aga Khan Award master jury recognises how architecture and the built environment define the diverse and divergent paths that lead to the capacious *lifeworlds* of contemporary Muslim societies. Our challenge was to judge the complex negotiation that architecture represents between, on the one hand, the sense of satisfaction and belonging that a building – a home – provides and, on the other, worldly ambitions and affiliations that are unconstrained by the retaining wall, village boundary or national frontier. Of 343 nominations, we shortlisted 27 projects for on-site review, and from these selected nine projects for recognition. Rather than grouping these projects under a common theme, or attempting to weigh them against a strict measure of quality, we proposed a set of 'curatorial principles' to inform and guide us. We saw ourselves as curators who, by placing these diverse projects next to one another, hoped to convey a sense of their specific attributes, their locality, while also giving them a collective meaning. Here are some of the curatorial principles with which we attempted to transform the expectations associated with the award.

Muslim Societies/Muslim Realities:

It was our privilege to be faced with architectural projects that raised important issues about an *umma* that is democratic and dialogical. Many of the projects occupied the problematic terrain between traditional homes and diasporic movements, recognising that Muslim realities have come to be rooted in historical and social circumstances beyond their usual 'national' or traditional settings. This is not a repudiation of values and traditions but rather an opportunity for cultural revision and intercultural communication. Change and challenging circumstances are part of both worlds, but the composition of contemporaneity, the speed of transformation, the conflict of values and the contingencies of 'identity' and solidarity may well be different. How, then, should we evaluate a new housing scheme whose disposition of spaces harmoniously and homogeneously accommodates a community that is governed by patriarchal power and authority? Does architectural excellence allow us to judge what may or may not be considered, among different communities, to be the 'good life'? Such a dialogic inquiry, posed with a remarkable *concreteness and visibility*, might provide an alternative to the futile 'clash of civilisations'.

Restoration, Conservation and Contemporaneity:

In the past the award has been associated with the conservation and restoration of great Muslim monuments. The actual performance of juries belies this perception. Our discussions asked: Are techniques of conservation and repair antithetical to claims of contemporaneity? How should we weigh architectural practice and performance? Conservation and restoration need not be part of the impulse to preserve the past in the vitrines of time and memory – antiquities set in aspic! The lifespan of the materials that constitute ancient monuments argues against 'preservation', because as materials decay they have to be recreated. Technological skills must be relearned and re-taught to new generations of craftsmen, new chemicals and engineering techniques have to be invented *in relation to past techniques and technologies*. Restoration is a work in progress or, in the preferred words of the jury, a work in *process*.

Scale and Variety:

Contemporary Muslim 'reality' is not merely diverse or transitional, as the clichés of globalisation would have it. As a jury we were challenged to adjust our critical and conceptual lenses as we moved across the landscape of the *umma* and its architectural artefacts and practices. *Scale* is not merely a problem internal to architectural knowledge or practice. The *scale* of the contemporary *umma* reveals profound differences in sites and localities – rural communities, small towns, industrial cities, private homes, public institutions – that demand both imagination and material, practical interventions. Scale is an architectural *intervention* that responds to site-specificity while at the same time creating or constructing a sense of *locality*. In that sense, *scale* is an ethical issue.

Sustainability:

Sustainability pits the grandiosity of our ambitions against the available and appropriate scale of natural resources. How high should we build? How suitable are our schemes for this particular landscape, climate, need or human interest? Sustainability, as a *scale* of aesthetic, ethical and political judgement, creates an architecture that is not just about building or *buildings*, but about creating an environment for survival and well-being, shared expression and solidarity, that is intolerant of authoritarian and exclusive claims to sovereignty.

Our sense of architectural 'excellence' demanded a scrutiny of the *singularity* of each project – its materials, its design solutions, its conceptual and physical realisation, its functional attributes – while creating a larger *aspectual* narrative that revealed different 'faces' which related to and reflected off one another. As *curators* we chose projects to be placed beside each other, juxtaposed so as to convey specificity, locality and something more – a shared community of excellence.

Homi K. Bhabha, Okwui Enwezor, Homa Farjadi, Sahel Al-Hiyari, Shirazeh Houshiary, Rashid Khalidi, Brigitte Shim, Han Tümertekin, Kenneth Yeang

Geneva, June 2007

Rehabilitation of the Walled City,
Nicosia, Cyprus

Samir Kassir Square
Beirut, Lebanon

Rehabilitation of the City of Shibam
Shibam, Yemen

Restoration of Amiriya Complex
Rada, Yemen

Central Market
Koudougou, Burkina Faso

Royal Netherlands Embassy
Addis Ababa, Ethiopia

14

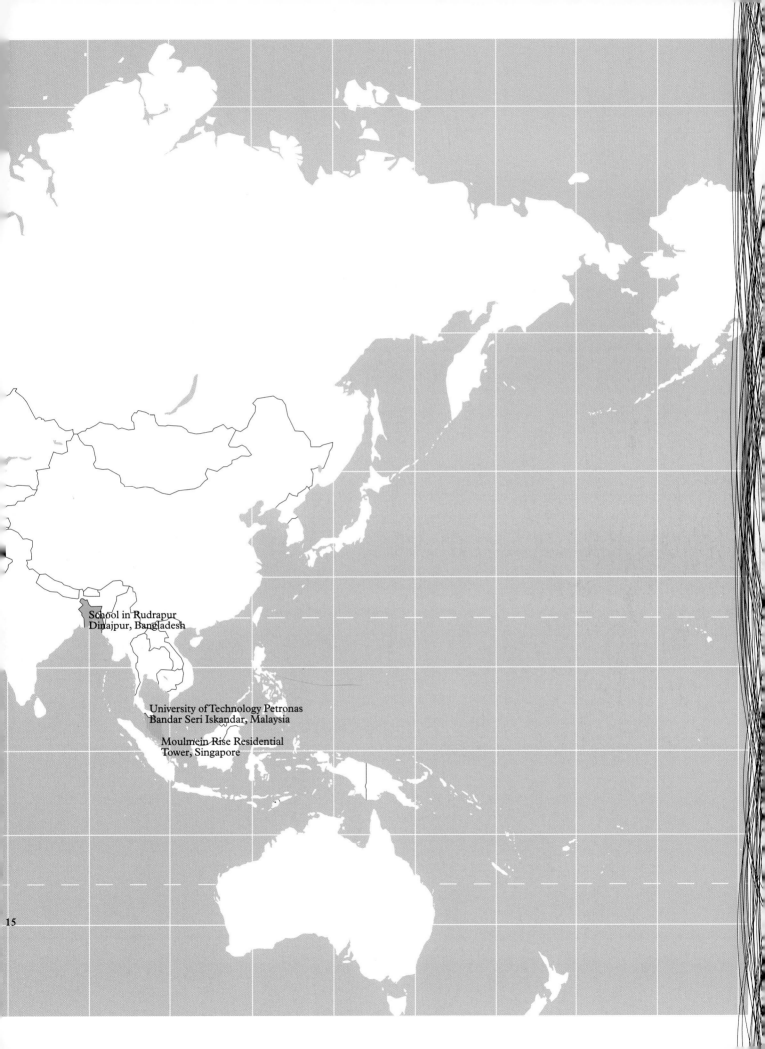

School in Rudrapur
Dinajpur, Bangladesh

University of Technology Petronas
Bandar Seri Iskandar, Malaysia

Moulmein Rise Residential
Tower, Singapore

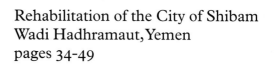

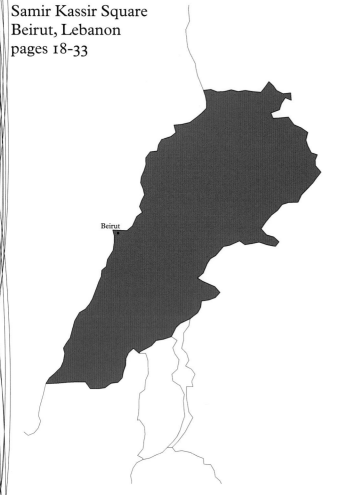

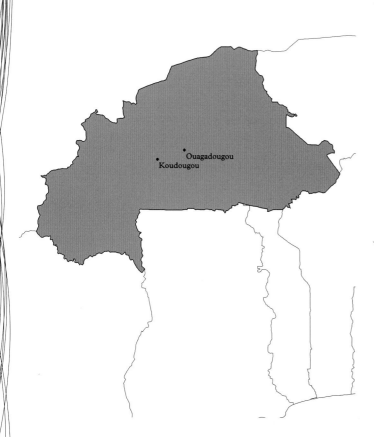

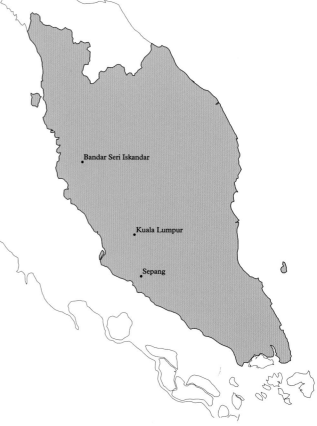

Aga Khan Award for Architecture 10th Cycle

Samir Kassir Square

Beirut
Lebanon

Vladimir Djurovic
Landscape Architecture

Introduction

Samir Kassir Square lies in the midst of Beirut's Central Business District, bordered on three sides by buildings and by a street on the fourth. Despite its frenetic setting, it is a place of calm and peace. At its heart are two old ficus trees, large enough to shade most of the space. A reflecting pool with water cascading over its edges marks the border between the square and the street. The pool is flanked by a raised timber deck that encircles the trees and supports a long bench of solid stone. The western side of the square is a bermed area that accommodates the downward slope of the site. The berm has a ground cover of dwarf Natal plum (*carissa macrocarpa*), a water-conserving plant known for its dark evergreen leaves and its white star-shaped flowers and red berries which grow throughout the year.

Jury Citation

One could read Samir Kassir Square simply as a stone bench, a wooden deck and a reflecting pool designed for the sole purpose of providing a visual frame for two of the oldest trees in downtown Beirut. Another possible reading would be that of a highly crafted and complex urban artefact which skillfully tackles the spatial conditions and infrastructure of its locality with a few calculated moves. The strength of the project is that it is purposefully situated between the two readings, in a state of restrained and silent complexity.

It is through the rigorous design approach and an economy of elements and language that the project achieves its objectives. The insistence on showing only what is essential – and nothing else – is what makes this particular work excel. One can trace a harmonious and logical thread that links the general idea to the detail, the architecture to the landscape, and the space to the city.

The importance of this work lies not only in the assimilation and transformation of its context, but also in what it necessitates, or rather how it actually transforms. This project conceives the public urban space as a shift in the city's rhythm. It emerges as a contemplative space where the diverse is celebrated, and allowed to exist in serene silence.

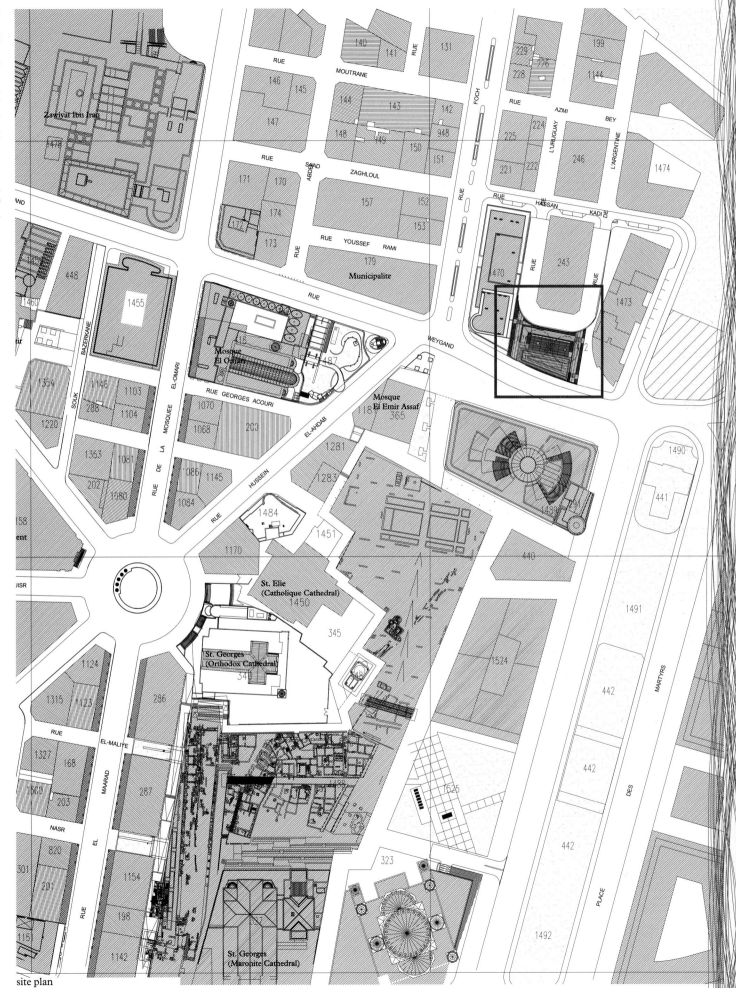

Zawiyat Ibn Iraq

RUE MOUTRANE

RUE SAAD ZAGHLOUL

RUE YOUSSEF RAMI

Municipalite

Mosque El Omari

RUE GEORGES ACOURI

RUE DE LA MOSQUEE

SOUK BAZERKANE

RUE EL-AHDAB

RUE HUSSEIN

Mosque El Emir Assaf

WEYGAND

FOCH

RUE AZMI BEY

L'URUGUAY

L'ARGENTINE

RUE HASSAN KADI

St. Elie
(Catholique Cathedral)

St. Georges
(Orthodox Cathedral)

RUE EL-MALIYE

EL MAARAD

NASR

RUE EL

MARTYRS

PLACE DES

St. Georges
(Maronite Cathedral)

site plan

Project Description

Solidere, the Lebanese Company for Development and Reconstruction, has been rebuilding the war-torn central area of Beirut since the mid-1990s. The company, Lebanon's largest, operates as a land and real-estate developer and a property manager. It has been granted powers of eminent domain as well as a level of regulatory authority subject to some controls, such as the granting of construction permits by the Beirut Municipality. Over the last decade it has commissioned new structure from both Lebanese architects and international practices such as Ricardo Bofill, Kohn Pedersen Fox, Steven Holl, Rafael Moneo, Jean Nouvel and Christian de Portzamparc.

The masterplan that Solidere developed for the Central Business District includes a number of public spaces, of which Samir Kassir Square is one. Occupying a site of 815 square metres, the square provides a space of greenery, shade and calm within a busy urban setting. Directly to its north is the an-Nahar newspaper and publishing house. To the west is the Beirut Municipality building, which dates back to the early part of the twentieth century and is currently being rehabilitated. The building to the south, now under construction, will house the headquarters of the National Bank of Kuwait as well as retail spaces and coffee shops. Another new building, a hotel, is rising to the east. In the very near future, then, the site will be completely surrounded by buildings, which will make its role as an open space even more vital.

Solidere initially considered cutting down the two old trees, as ficus are notorious for their invasive root system and extensive shedding of leaves. The architect dissuaded them, and instead masterfully incorporated them into the design. He argued that the trees are amongst the few mature specimens surviving in the area, and are an expression of the history and memory of the place. They also have a powerful inherent sculptural quality that makes them the main visual focus of the square.

The area around the two trees is covered with a raised timber deck made of Burma teak planks. This raised deck serves a number of purposes. It separates the floor from the root systems of the ficus, which can break on-grade pavements made of concrete or stone. It also protects the trees: the more usual practice of adding layers of earth to the original ground level to cover the root system carries the risk of suffocating them. In addition, the use of the raised deck creates space underneath for the mechanical room housing the pumps and filters for the pool.

The reflecting, cascading pool provides an element of separation from the busy street flanking the site on the east, helping to create an intimate and contemplative space. The sound of the water brimming over the pool's grooved edges has a soothing effect and creates a counterbalance to the noise of the surrounding city. The reflecting surface of the pool mirrors part of the surroundings, creating a sense of expansiveness.

Vladimir Djurovic's work is known for its meticulous detailing and emphasis on durability, and he generally focuses on a limited palette of materials in each of his designs. At Samir Kassir Square, he accentuates hard-scaping (primarily stone) with plant materials. Local basalt pebbles line the inside of the pool, and imported Italian Bardelio stone is used for the sides, since no local stone could be found with the requisite characteristics of colour and reflectivity. Local Kour limestone is used for the floor paving, the long bench and the steps. The latter are made from solid stone blocks rather than a reinforced concrete skeleton sheathed in paving – this solution, although more expensive in the short term, will better resist extensive wear and tear.

The large ficus trees and the pool create a very pleasant cool and shaded microclimate within the centre of Beirut, a place to escape the heat of the summer months. Many who work in this part of the CBD come to the garden in search of peace and quiet. The square is especially popular with the staff of the an-Nahar newspaper.

Originally known as Square Four, the space was renamed Samir Kassir Public Garden after the assassination of the popular intellectual and an-Nahar columnist Samir Kassir in June 2005. His widow, Gizelle Khoury, campaigned to have the square renamed in his honour, since he was known to be fond of the space and liked to spend time there.

In the way it draws people towards it, the square highlights the positive role that public spaces can play as places of refuge, calm and contemplation – at a time when many of the public spaces in our cities are being programmed primarily for leisure and recreation.

In its visual conception, in its sparing use of materials and forms and in the quality of its detailing, the garden points to a clear new direction for landscape design in a region where the discipline is not yet well established or mature, and where designers often try to emulate prototypes (such as tropical, English or French gardens) that are inappropriate and out of context, both visually and environmentally.

Text adapted from a report
by Mohammad al-Asad

site plan

1 solid stone bench
2 wooden deck
3 ficus trees
4 reflecting pool
5 entrances

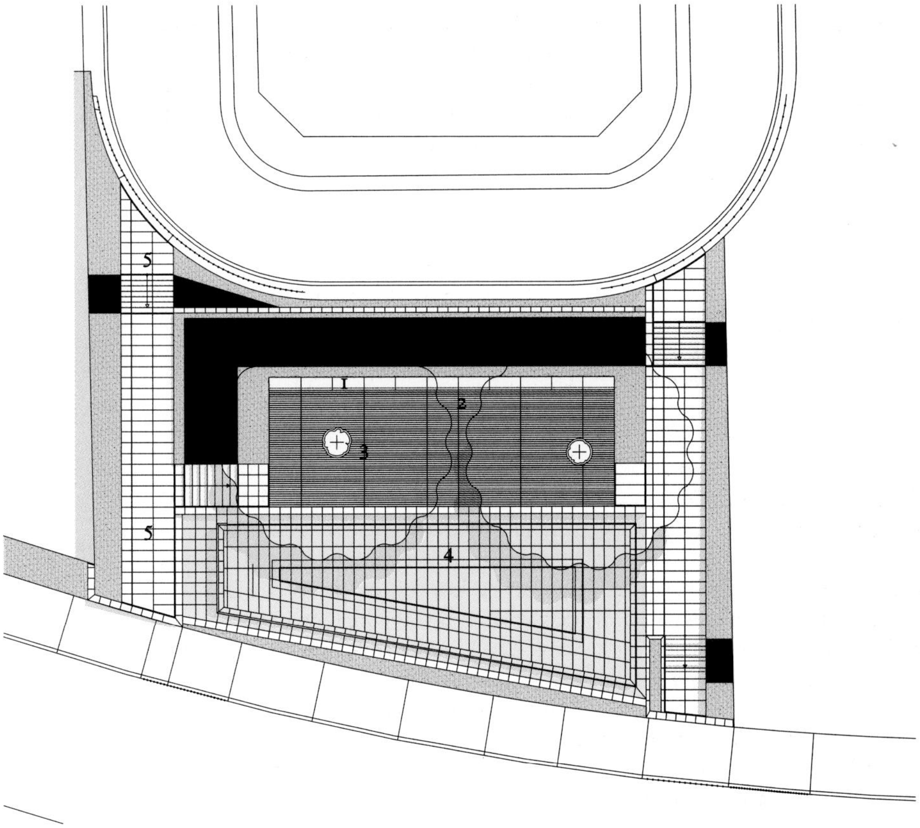
5
1
2
3
5
4

elevation

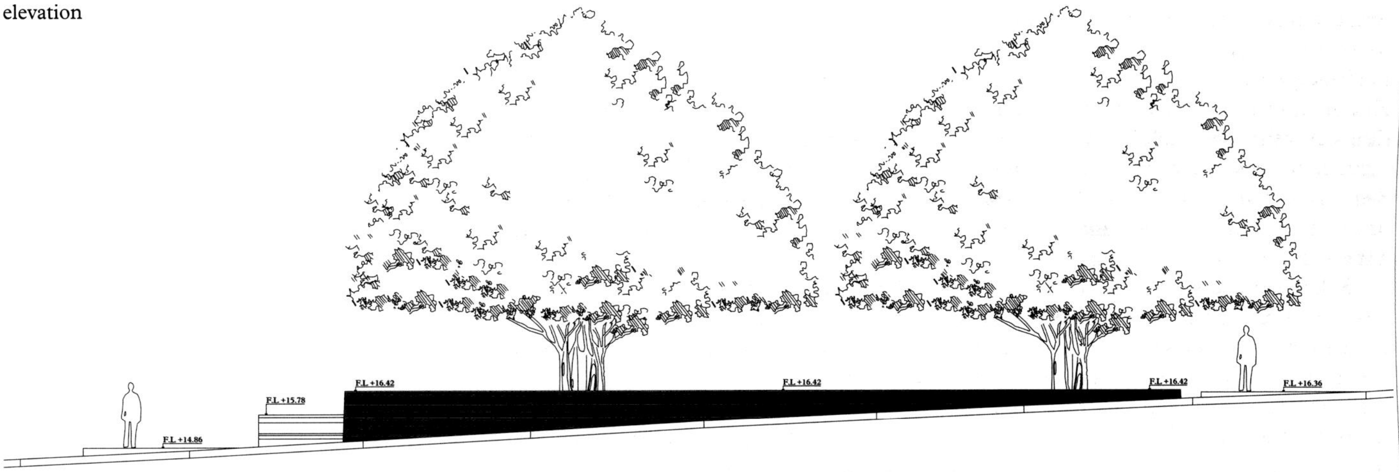
F.L +15.78
F.L +14.86
F.L +16.42
F.L +16.42
F.L +16.42
F.L +16.36

section

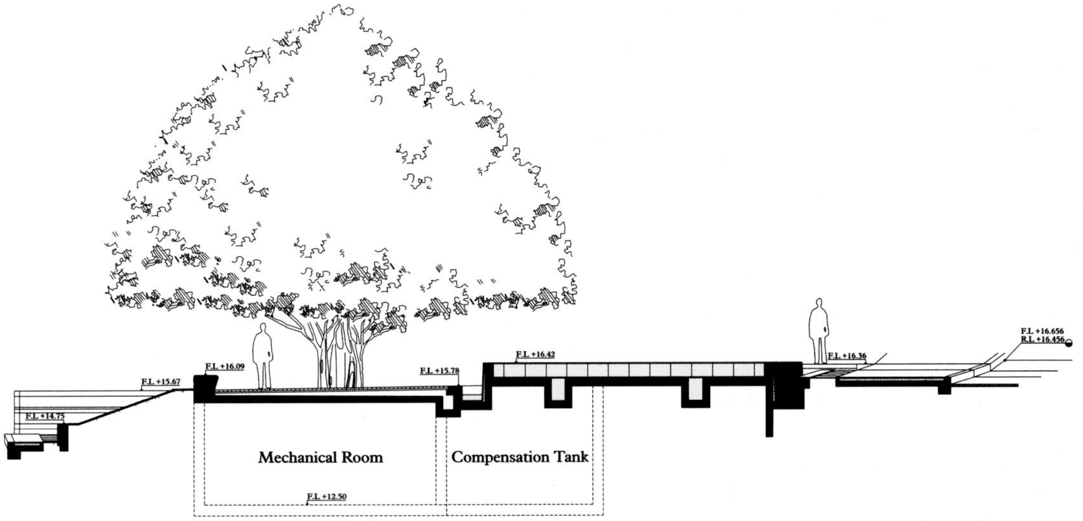
F.L +16.09
F.L +15.67
F.L +14.75
F.L +15.78
F.L +16.42
F.L +16.36
F.L +16.656
R.L +16.456
Mechanical Room
Compensation Tank
F.L +12.50

Samir Kassir Square
Weygand Street, Beirut, Lebanon

Client
Solidere (Société Libanaise de Développement et Reconstruction), Lebanon: Nasser Shamma, chairman and general manager; Subhi Rifai, project manager

Architect
Vladimir Djurovic Landscape Architecture, Lebanon: Vladimir Djurovic, principal; Paul De Mar Yousef, design architect; Salim Kanaan, project architect

Contractor
AG Contracting, Lebanon

Lighting Designer
Light Box, Lebanon

Water Engineer
Hydrelec, Lebanon

Project Data
Site area: 815 m²
Costs: US$ 322,000
Commission: July 2002
Design: July 2002–October 2002
Construction: November 2002–May 2004
Occupancy: May 2004

Websites
www.solidere.com/solidere.html
www.vladimirdjurovic.com

Lebanese architect Vladimir Djurovic established the Beirut-based Vladimir Djurovic Landscape Architecture (VDLA) in 1995. The firm offers a full range of landscape architectural services with all their architectural and interior complements. Its expertise extends from the creation of getaways and retreats to the planning and development of boutique hotels and resorts, from private residences to intricate urban spaces. Djurovic has been successful in architectural competitions and has won a series of awards, including the American Society of Landscape Architects' Residential Design Award of Excellence for the Elie Saab Residence in Lebanon in 2007 and a Cityscape Architectural Review Award in 2005. He has lectured at Imperial College London and the Architectural Association of Ireland and his work has been featured in many international journals and magazines.

Beirut, Square Four

Rehabilitation of the City of Shibam

Wadi Hadhramaut
Yemen

GTZ Technical Office
GOPHCY

Introduction

The mud-brick high-rise buildings of Shibam cluster in a walled
mass that exudes the genius of Yemeni architecture. As an urban
monument, Shibam is of international architectural significance,
yet the motor of this rehabilitation project is not the preservation
of buildings but rather the creation of new economic and social
structures that will restore the vitality of the city. A joint Yemeni-
German initiative, the Shibam Urban Development Project has
stemmed depopulation by providing technical and financial support
for the renovation of almost half of the housing stock. It has worked
with the local authorities to improve essential services and infrastructure. Most importantly, it has given local people the means and
the confidence to take concrete steps towards improving their lives.
Through new community-based organisations local craftsmen are
being trained, women are being offered literacy classes and the chance
to learn new skills, and agriculture in the outlying area is being revived
through the restoration of the old canal and spate irrigation system.

Jury Citation

Over the course of two decades, a number
of agencies and individuals have committed
time and resources not simply to preserve
the unique urban and architectural heritage
of the ancient city of Shibam, but also to
establish a viable alternative to the mun-
dane mass architecture found in many
economically depressed parts of the world.
In restoring nearly 200 houses and dis-
seminating social services, the Urban
Development Project has approached the
city as a living community rather than a
historical artefact frozen in time.

Through the efforts of NGOs, architects
and stakeholders, Shibam has eluded
imminent obsolescence under the amnesiac
pressures of globalisation, growing into
a platform for the reinvention of the vernacular high-rise in twenty-first century
conditions. Located on the threshold
between past and present, tradition and
modernity, this walled city of vertical mud-
brick high-rises, with its labyrinthine streets
and lanes, unfolds its own iterative narrative
in a stunning, almost oneiric topography.
All these efforts have allowed the citizens
to re-imagine their city beyond its sheer
liminality in the cosmopolitan discourse
of contemporary urbanism.

restored private
owned houses
restored
(AWGAF owned)
restored public
buildings &
monuments

valuable houses
restored
ruins (33u)

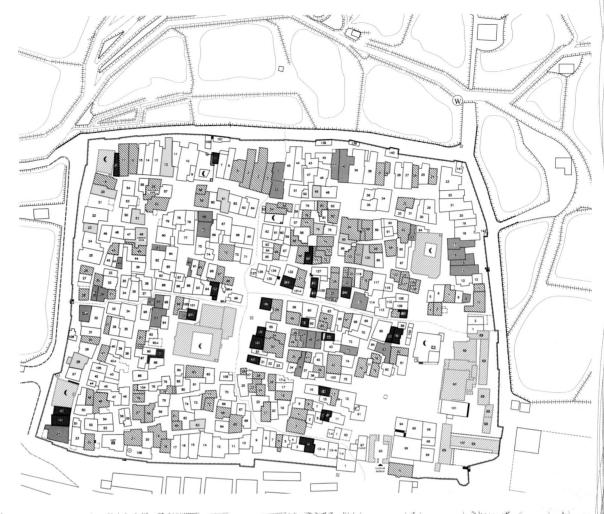

priority interventions
required
ruins
limits of degraded
zones in 2006

restored houses
through SHHP
degraded zones
before restoration
through SHHP

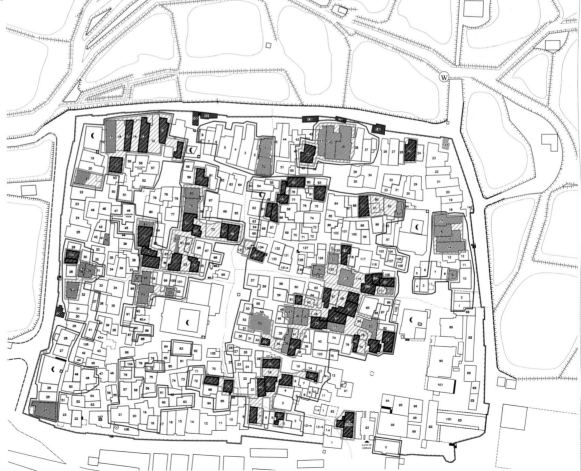

Project Description

Shibam is one of the few historic cities of the Hadhramaut valley that is not built directly against a mountain backdrop. Instead, it sits on a raised earth dais thought to be the rubble of an ancient city, and is surrounded by a city wall. Along with Seyoun and Tarim, it is one of major urban centres in Hadhramaut. In times past it was also the commercial capital where caravans assembled on the Arabia trade route. Although there is no definite date for the construction of Shibam, its name is mentioned in early texts and in pre-Islamic poetry (Umru' al Qais). The older buildings date back 200 to 300 years, and they have been repeatedly reconstructed over the centuries to sustain the architectural mass and volume of the city.

The vertical expansion of the buildings was informed by the topography and by the need to preserve the surrounding agricultural land. The ground floors of houses in this region are traditionally taken up with grain and staple food storage. In Shibam the ground and first floors have dark and lofty depots with few openings for ventilation. Sheep and goats are kept in adjacent rooms and terraces on the first floor at night. The second and third floors are occupied by several living rooms (mahadir) used by the men, while the fourth and fifth floors contain living areas for the women, along with kitchens, washrooms and toilet facilities. The sixth and upper floors are used by children or by newlyweds in the extended family. Terraces placed at the upper levels make up for the lack of open courtyards in the house.

When the Urban Development Project started in 2000, many of these houses were in danger of collapse and people were leaving the city. Improvements to the housing stock had to be a matter of priority. An economist, Burkhard von Rabenau, was asked to analyse possible ways of assisting owners to carry out the necessary improvements to their houses. He suggested that the people of Shibam were being indirectly taxed for living in a listed site, since they were denied development rights and the option of building to lower standards. To offset this situation, it seemed appropriate to offer a subsidy. The proposal was discussed with the Social Fund for Development of Yemen, which agreed to fund the subsidies provided they were offered on a clear and transparent basis, with residents contributing their fair share, and that the work involved a strong training component, benefiting the local workforce.

As a matter of principle, the project insists that owners take charge of the restoration of their property – that they actively set their own priorities for the intervention, commission the master builder of their choice, and manage the construction budget. Subsidies are given directly to the owners in stages, as the work progresses.

To date almost 200 houses have been restored, along with a number of public buildings and monuments including mosques, historic fountains, watchtowers and the city gate. The project followed the advice of senior master builders in treating structural problems in the mud buildings. Responses include adding wooden stilts (ma'atin) along damaged facades to help reduce the load of the upper floors, using horizontal wooden beams to 'stitch' vertical cracks in walls, replacing defective structural elements, and in extreme cases removing added floors to reduce the extra loads imposed on the buildings. All of these structural interventions are traditionally practised in Shibam, though it was necessary to engage senior master builders to supervise the work of the younger builders and train them in these techniques.

All structural elements are made from ilb, a local hardwood, except in extreme cases where the upper floors are supported by steel tubes (a method used in spanning ceilings in mud brick building in Hadhramaut since the 1980s). Renderings are usually made from mud mixed with local hay and straw. Alluvial mud is collected from the agricultural fields around the city after every few floods. This returns the fields to their original level, and the funds raised from the sale of the mud are used to maintain the irrigation system. For waterproofing the outer surfaces of the building, lime is applied in two layers followed by a final wash. The first application is thick while the second layer is thinner and is usually mixed, while wet, with fine sand that acts as aggregate to stabilise the lime. The final lime wash is usually mixed with a small quantity of red sugar.

Yet the restoration of the built fabric is just one strand of the programme. The other vital components are the mobilising of community-based organisations and the initiating of interventions based on community participation and priorities. In this way, the economic and social impact of the project has extended beyond the historic city, reaching the whole district of Shibam through the organisations it has helped set up.

The Hawtah Women's Charity and Social Association runs literacy programmes, classes in sewing, hairdressing and computing, and a scholarship programme enabling young high-school graduates to go to university in the nearby town of Seyoun.

The Hazm Community Centre provides workshops for women living in extreme poverty. A core unit of around 35 women is currently adapting traditional weaving techniques to create more lucrative products for the tourist market.

The Agricultural Cooperative Association is based on the old tradition of the water rights committee and brings together about 80 per cent of the farmers and landowners in the spate irrigation lands around the historic city. Working with the project, the association is coordinating the rehabilitation of the intricate irrigation system.

The Mud Architecture Association, with some 33 active master builders and 220 workers and apprentices on its register, oversees all the restoration work supported by the project. The association negotiates salaries of workers and apprentices and has also established a social security fund to compensate workers who are injured on site. The demand for skilled labour in the city has quadrupled since the project's inception.

Inspired by the success of these organisations, other community groups have launched their own initiatives and sought the project's assistance to implement programmes. Local schools are organising lessons in traditional crafts, a music ensemble is reviving musical traditions to pass them on to younger generations, a private museum has set up a workshop training high-school students to build models of Shibami houses, local craftspeople are developing new products to sell to tourists, a cultural club has organised a travelling exhibition of historic photographs, and so on. The project is ongoing. What has been achieved so far highlights the importance of Shibam as a living site rather than a museum – a place where the inhabitants are developing and modernising the structures that improve everyday life, creating a contemporary setting with their urban heritage.

Text adapted from a report
by Salma Samar Damluji

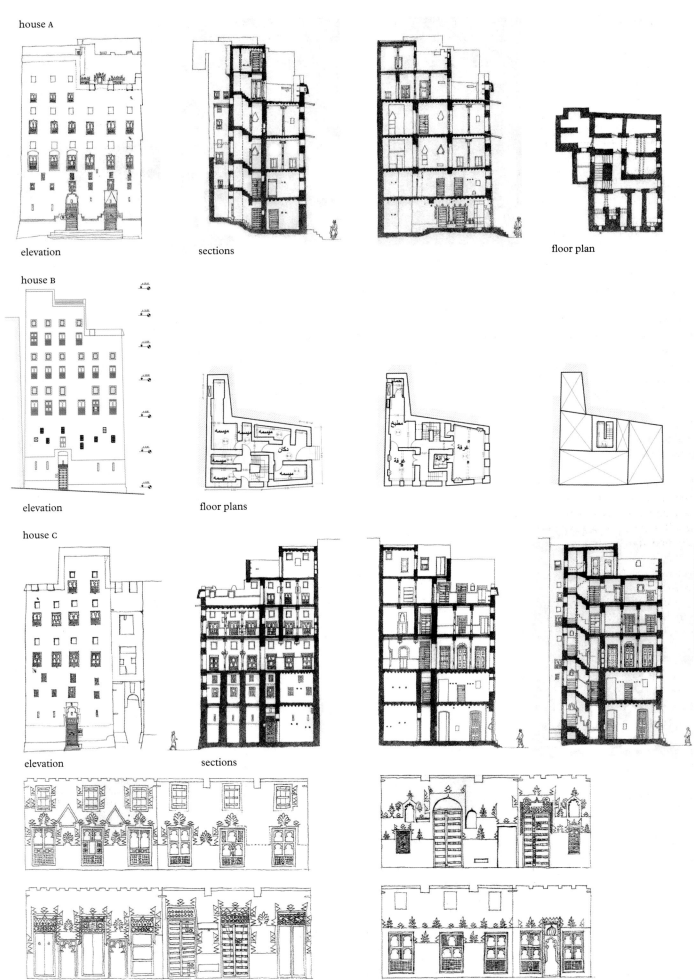

house A

elevation   sections   floor plan

house B

elevation   floor plans

house C

elevation   sections

interior elevations

Rehabilitation of the City of Shibam

Shibam, Governorate of Hadhramaut, Yemen

Client
German Federal Ministry of Economic Cooperation (BMZ), Germany; Ministry of Culture, Yemen; local community, Shibam

Local Council: Tariq Talib Falhum, director general, Shibam District; Mari'i Badr Jabiri, secretary general; Hud Bazurais, Shibam representative

Implementing Agencies
General Organisation for the Preservation of Historic Cities of Yemen (GOPHCY): Abdullah Zaid Ayssa, director (2006–2007); Abdullah Bawazir, director (2000–2005). German Technical Cooperation (GTZ), Sana'a: Thomas Engelhardt, director (2007); Helmut Grosskreutz, director (2000–2006). GTZ Shibam office: Omar Abdulaziz Hallaj, team leader (2004–2007); Ursula Eigel, team leader (2000–2004)

Other Sponsors
Social Fund for Development, Yemen; German Development Services (DED), Germany

Architects and Engineers
GTZ and DED: Omar Abdulaziz Hallaj (GTZ), development of housing programme/project support; Tom Liermann (DED), historic features programme and training for technical unit; Mohamad al-Kaderi (GTZ), management of technical unit (2002-2005); Erik Schweikhardt (GTZ), support for technical unit; Martin Zeifert (DED), plumbing and infrastructure expert
GOPHCY: Jamal Bamakhrama, management of GOPHCY contribution; Sadiq al-Mashhour, management of technical unit (2006); Ali Baraja, field architect; Mazin Sheikh al-Masawi, field engineer

Administration
Khalid Gaashan (GTZ), project officer/planner

Documentation and Archiving
Monaf Abboud and Abdullah Sabain (GOPHCY)

Consultants
Burkhard von Rabenau, economist; Hadi Saliba, conservation planning; Jamal Jaber, wood conservation; Khaled Sharif and Nabil al-Jerafi, solid waste management; Nadim Rahmoun, infrastructure implementation

Community Development Officers
Aisha Said, senior community development officer (2000-2004); Hana Bin Taleb and Eshraq Aidan, community development officers; Amina Bin Taleb, junior community development expert (all GTZ)

Principal Master Builders
Housing Programme: Said Baswatayn, supervisor; Monuments Fund projects: Jam'an Basaida, Mbarak al Juraydi and Awad Huwaydi, supervisors. Mud Architecture Association: Salem Awad Msawnaq, chair (2007); Faraj Salim Kwayran, chair (2005–2007); Senior Master Builders' Committee: Salem Msawnaq, Ubayd Basawatayn, Salem al Hadri, Jama'an Basaida, Mahfuz Huwaidi, members

Master Builders (Housing and Monument Restoration)
Ali Marbash, Faraj Kwairan, Saleh Bahdaila, Kamal al-Hadri, Hazmi al-Hadri, Khairan Bayashout, Mahfouz Bahdaila, Mohamad Baswaitin, Omar al-Hadri, Faraj Badawi, Awad Baziad, Ahmad Bayashout, Ashour Kwairan, Said Wadaan, Ahmad Houwaidi, Ali Bakrbashat, Jum'an Mouzaynan, Ahmad Badawi, Awad Wad'an

Master Carpenters
Ahmad Bajidah, Omar Bajidah, Mahfuz Bajidah, Sabri Kharaz, Fadil Bajidah, Ahmad Baya'shut, Brik Zubair, Ali Zoubair

Project Data
Site area: 81,000 m²
Cost: US$ 4,000,000 (calculated December 2006)
Commission: January 2000
Design: 2000–2006
Construction: 2000–2006
Completed: 2005 (new phase ongoing)

Websites
www.gtz.de
www.shibam-udp.org

The German Technical Cooperation Agency (GTZ) is an international cooperation enterprise commissioned by the German Federal Ministry of Economic Cooperation (BMZ) to implement technical development cooperation programmes worldwide. Yemen is a priority partner country and GTZ has been active there since 1969. BMZ also sponsors the German Development Services (DED) to place seconded experts with development partners.

The General Organisation for the Preservation of Historic Cities of Yemen (GOPHCY) was established in 1984 as the organisation responsible for the preservation of the urban fabric of the Old City of Sana'a. The scope of its mandate was later enlarged to include all of Yemen, and it is the state authority for historic preservation of urban heritage, reporting to the Ministry of Culture.

The Social Fund for Development is a Yemeni organisation established in 1997 as a major component in the national social safety net. It implements community development programmes to improve people's access to basic services, and works to create an enabling environment for small and micro enterprises.

The Shibam Urban Development Project was initiated in 2000 through the efforts of Ursula Eigel (team leader 2000–2004). After completing her studies in law and social sciences in Frankfurt, Munich and Paris, she joined GTZ in 1975, directing urban programmes in Zambia, Jordan, Yemen and Nepal among many other countries. She was the team leader for the GTZ project on government reform in Kenya from 1988 to 1996.

The project's current team leader, Omar Abdulaziz Hallaj, is a Syrian architect trained at the University of Texas at Austin, where he received both his bachelor's and Master's degrees. Hallaj works on urban development, planning and heritage conservation. Prior to his work in Shibam, he had a private architectural practice in Aleppo, Syria, where he also served as the chairperson of the technical committee responsible for the preservation of the Old City of Aleppo.

43

Central Market

Koudougou
Burkina Faso

The Swiss Agency for Development
and Cooperation (SDC) /
Laurent Séchaud

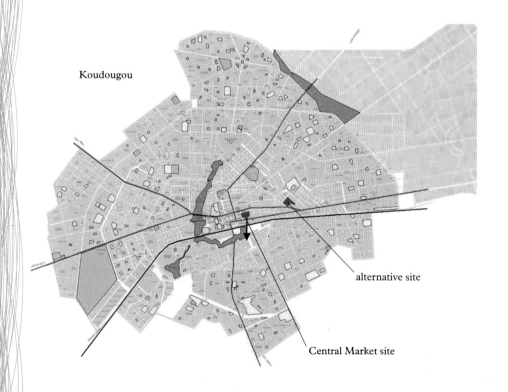

Koudougou

alternative site

Central Market site

Introduction

This impact of Koudougou Central Market is twofold. At the urban scale, it reinforces and enhances the fabric of a mid-sized town, providing a place for commercial and social exchange. On the level of construction, it introduces simple and easily assimilated improvements to a traditional material – stabilised earth – that allow it to achieve its full aesthetic and environmental potential.

The market is the third of its type to be built under the direction of Swiss Agency for Development and Cooperation (SDC). It capitalises on the experience gained at Fada N'Gourma and Ouahigouya, turning trial techniques into practical solutions. The construction of the nearby spice market (also supported by the SDC) was used as a training ground for the workforce, as well as a pilot project for the participatory process that shaped the design of the Central Market – and continues to determine its operation today.

Jury Citation

The Central Market responds sensitively to its urban context while also creating powerful sculptural spaces in its interior. Blocks of compressed earth are used to form celebratory domes, vaults and arches, demonstrating how large repetitive structural spans have the capacity to ennoble public space.

The building of a 1:1 prototype of a typical retail space facilitated communication between the different collaborators, simultaneously allowing refinement of the design, development of innovative construction techniques and practical training of the local masons. More than just a piece of physical urban infrastructure in a mid-sized town, this project is the result of a truly participatory process that brought together and engaged the entire community in the site selection, design and construction of the market as well as its continuing use. With simple means, the project has shaped a monumental civic space for meeting and exchange.

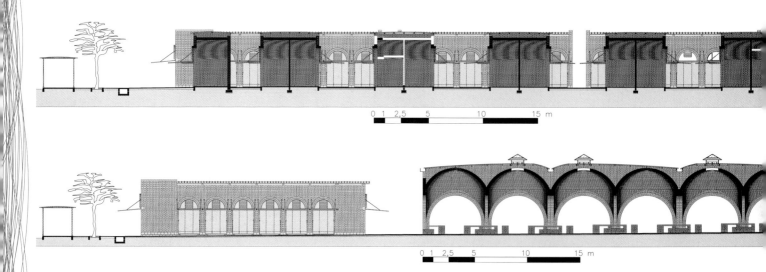

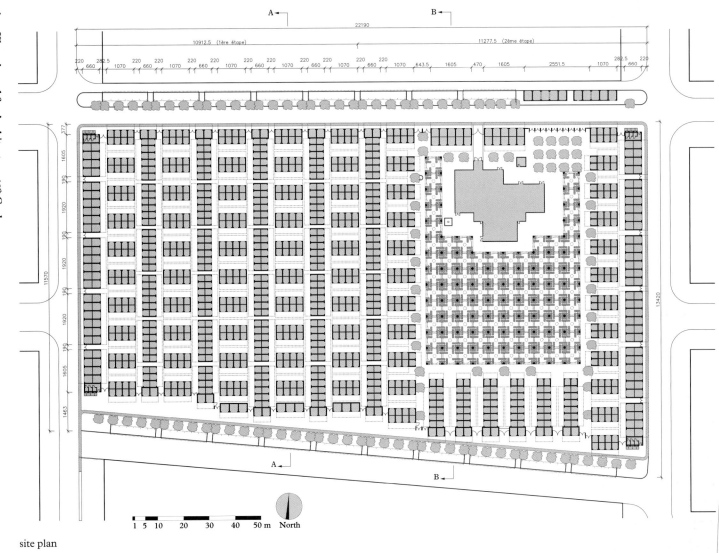

site plan

1 5 10   20   30   40   50 m   North

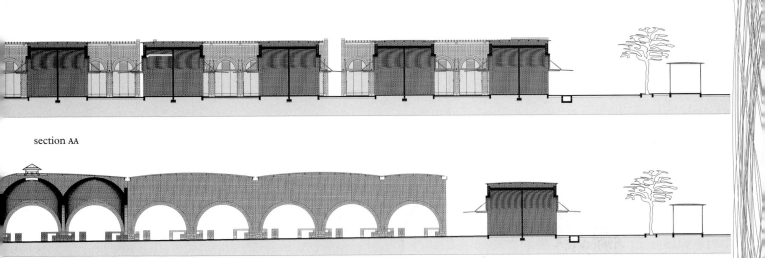

section AA

section BB

Project Description

Burkina Faso is being indelibly changed by rapid urbanisation. Not long ago, 90 per cent of the population lived in rural areas, scattered across more than 8,000 villages. Now there is a seemingly unstoppable flow of migration to the country's two largest urban centres, and in particular the capital Ouagadougou. In an effort to balance the effects of this rural exodus, the government launched the PDVM (Programme de Développement des Villes Moyennes) in 1990. The programme's aim is to strengthen the country's mid-sized towns by using commercial infrastructures such as markets, bus stations and slaughterhouses as the driving force for a sustainable development. Swiss support of the programme began in 1992, through the SDC (Swiss Agency for Development and Cooperation).

With a population of 75,000 inhabitants, Koudougou is the third largest city in the country. It combines a grandiose colonial gridiron layout of wide streets with a modest building typology that adapts a rural model to the urban context. One-storey compounds – the homes of extended families – consist of rectangular rooms arranged around a central open space. Once built of earth blocks (banco), they are now mainly of concrete. In fact, almost all new domestic construction uses imported building materials, and the traditional straw roofing has been replaced with corrugated zinc sheets. All the main administrative buildings and other urban facilities are also concrete-block construct-ions. Concrete is generally seen as more durable and therefore more desirable, despite its higher cost.

By using stabilised earth, the market not only demonstrates the superior climatic performance of the local building material, but also shows how humble earth blocks can be used to create a sophisticated pattern language of vaults, domes and arches.

The project for the Central Market was conceived in 1997. A bilateral project committee was officially established in June 1999; it had twelve members, including six storekeepers and future beneficiaries of the new project, and an architect representing the SDC. It took the committee about five months to construct a programme and translate it into an architectural scheme that satisfied all the partners. The shopkeepers wanted to stay on the existing site, rather than move to a proposed new, larger location a kilometre away. The planned solution was therefore to have a very dense market, with a maximum number of permanent individual shops (of six square metres each). In total, the new market was to provide 1,155 shops, 624 stalls and two administrative buildings as well as the necessary ancillary services such as public toilets and water taps.

The detailed architectural project was adopted in December 2000 after the construction of a 1:1 model of a retail shop. The prototype was necessary to avoid misunderstandings, as most committee members did not know how to read architectural drawings. It also allowed for the testing of various constructional and structural aspects, and resulted in a number of modifications to the design: the thickness of some lateral walls was reduced from 45 to 30 centimetres; the height of the arches was raised; and the vaults were reconsidered, with adjustments made to the quantity of mortar. The prototype also gave a good indication of the real costs of the project. The quantity of materials was precisely calculated, and even the construction schedule was revised. The prototype was a kind of test-site that helped to assess the capabilities of the local labour force and identify training priorities.

Construction took place in two phases, from January 2001 to June 2002, and from May 2003 to June 2005. Earth for the blocks was manually extracted from a hill two kilometres from the site. Different shapes and sizes of block were developed for the needs of the project. A rigorous dimension-ing ensured they could be used whole, with no left-over parts; hence the block was used as the construction module.

The load-bearing walls are 29.5 centimetres thick and made of earth blocks stabilised with 4 to 12 per cent industrial cement, cast in hand presses on site and bound with an earth mortar. Partition walls are 14 centimetres thick, and also made of compressed earth blocks.

The market covers a total area of 29,000 square metres on a rectangular plot oriented roughly northwest to southeast. Around its periphery are shops that stay open beyond the general opening hours of the market, animating the city centre.

The market's internal layout is quite simple and regular. A first orthogonal grid, with rows of shops running east–west along the width of the market, defines the alleys. A second orthogonal grid – with shops directed north–south along its length – defines the small gathering places. The second grid is interrupted by an open, domed space supported by a series of high arches that contains the stalls. The juxtaposition of the two grids generates a special rhythm that disrupts the high density and repetitiveness of the construction. It also opens up views all along the length and breadth of the market. This organisation allows for good air circulation and gives every building the benefit of shade created by the other constructions. Solar exposure is minimised.

Compressed earth blocks, traditionally used only for walls, are used here for roofs as well. At first, these were conceived in the form of domes, but a comparative study showed that vaults were a more straight-forward solution for such a large-scale structure. The one exception is in the stalls zone, where dome-shaped roofs accommo-date the longer spans that are necessary to allow easy circulation between the tables and stools. In total, the project incorporates 85 domes, 658 vaults and 1,425 arches, all constructed without the use of formwork, as timber is a precious resource in this region.

Corrugated metal sheets were used to make the earthen roofs and domes more waterproof, thus reducing the need for frequent repair and helping to counter the preconception that stabilised earth is costly to maintain. There is a gap of about 35 centimetres between the domes and the corrugated metal sheets to allow air to circulate and improve the interior climate.

The structural use of wood was limited to the beams used to fix the corrugated metal sheets. Steel was used for gates, louvres and doors, in keeping with local practice apart from one major innovation – the introduction of counterweighted top-hinged doors that cover the whole shop front when closed, and form a canopy over the street when open. Reinforced concrete was used only for the foundations, for the underground water tank and for the slab covering the sewage system.

Being labour-intensive, this project generated more jobs than a construction in concrete. The raw material was extracted by locals and all blocks were made on site at a rate of 1,000 bricks a day per worker. Training was also one of the key positive aspects. No less than 140 masons obtained their certification in the new techniques of constructing vaults, domes and arches without formwork. A few of these masons are women, who now work as freelance entrepreneurs.

The Central Market is part of a broader local development strategy. It was approached not as a conventional commercial activity, but as a participatory process engaging a wide cross-section of the community. The market continues to be run by a community-based organisation, while its integrative approach has been extended to other new development projects. The Public Establish-ment for Community Development, financed by the SDC, brings together seven of the town's ten sectors, each represented by its civic organisations and community leaders, and each with its own participatory development plan.

Text adapted from a report
by Naima Chabbi-Chemrouk

54

shop building

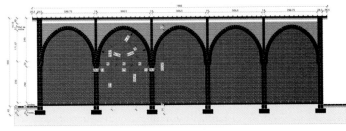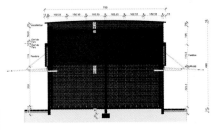

elevations

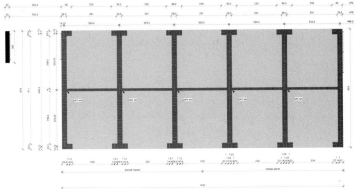

sections

floor plan

service building

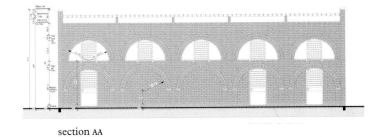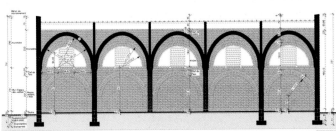

section AA section BB

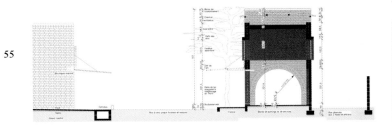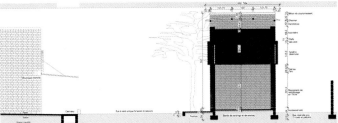

crossection crossection

Central Market
Koudougou, Burkina Faso

Client
Koudougou Municipality,
Burkina Faso

Sponsor
Swiss Agency for Development and
Cooperation

Architects
Swiss Agency for Development and
Cooperation: Laurent Séchaud,
principal architect, Burkina Faso;
Pierre Jéquier, consultant, France

Engineer
Etablissement Public Communal
pour le Développement, Burkina
Faso: Joseph P. Nikiema

Technician
Harouna Moyenga, Burkina Faso

Master Masons
Zanna Kientega, Mouboë Bado,
Kouka Bonkoungou, Michel T.
Zagre, Sanata Kabore, Victorine
Bonkoungou (all in Burkina Faso)

Project Data
Built area: 27,750 m²
Site area: 29,000 m²
Cost: US$ 2,470,000
Commission: June 1999
Design: August 1999–
September 2004
Construction: January 2001–
June 2005
Occupancy: June 2005

Bibliography
Thierry Joffroy, *Eléments de base sur la construction en arcs, voûtes et coupoles*, published by SKAT, Centre de Coopération Suisse pour la technologie et le management, St Gall, 1994

Websites
www.sdc.admin.ch
www.mairie-koudougou.bf/
lamunicipalite/epcd.html

The Swiss Agency for Development and Cooperation (SDC) is the agency responsible for the overall coordination of international development activities within the Swiss Foreign Ministry. Its aim is to alleviate poverty in partner countries by implementing projects that promote economic reform and governmental autonomy, helping people to help themselves. SDC's bilateral development cooperation concentrates on 17 priority countries and seven special programmes in Africa, Asia and Latin America. At the multi-national level, SDC collaborates with UN agencies, the World Bank and regional development banks.

Laurent Séchaud (b. 1967) completed his architectural studies at the University of Geneva in 1995. He worked on a variety of projects in urban planning and architecture before becoming involved with the Swiss Agency for Development and Cooperation (SDC) in Burkina Faso. He has been part of the Programme de Développement des Villes Moyennes (PDVM), a team working on making regional development hubs in medium-sized towns in the state of Burkinabe in Burkina Faso. His projects have included offices, markets, an abattoir, a bus station, institutional buildings and workshops. Apart from his work with SDC, he has also designed houses and a women's centre in Burkina Faso.

University of Technology Petronas

Bandar Seri Iskandar
Malaysia

Foster + Partners and
GDP Architects

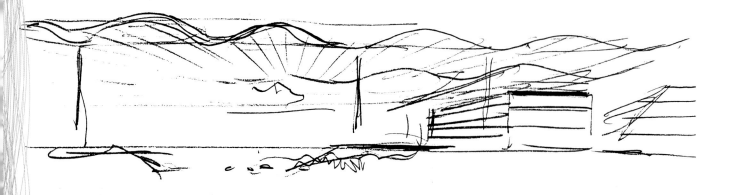

Introduction

Malaysia's sustained growth in recent decades is due in large part to the development of a strong education sector, one that aims especially to contribute to advances in the fields of science and technology. In support of this ambition, the government invited the petroleum company Petronas to set up a private university that would nurture technically qualified, well-rounded graduates who could direct the development of key industries in Malaysia. Blending academic training with hands-on experience, the University of Technology Petronas is conceived as an environment that will encourage creativity and innovation, 'a place to learn and not a place to be taught'.

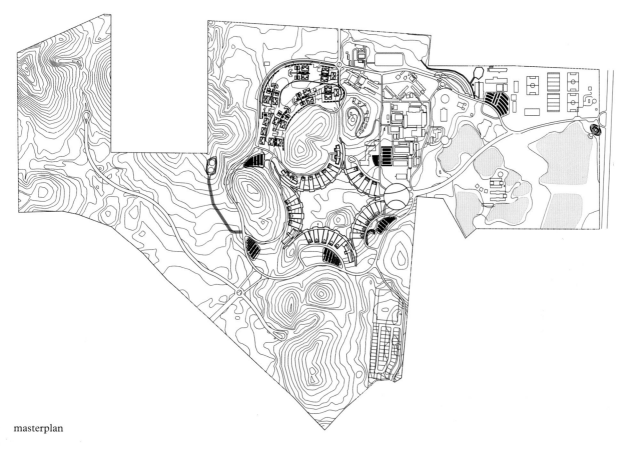

masterplan

Jury Citation

The project's significance lies in a number of aspects.

First, its prototypical built configuration, consisting of an all-encompassing shaped canopy with functional boxes inserted underneath, is a contemporary reinterpretation of the classic metaphor for tropical architecture – an umbrella that offers protection from the sun and rain.

Second, the building provides a defined shaded zone for social interaction and circulation under an overhead enclosure. This is a high-tech, emblematic architecture appropriate for a scientific university in a rapidly developing nation.

Third, the careful physical integration of a complex educational structure with the existing landscape is achieved in an ingenious way, by wrapping the built forms around the base of a series of knolls.

And fourth, this is an exemplary use of a performance-based approach to architectural design that goes beyond the diagram. The design has been carried through to completion with meticulous detail, rigour and persistence. It sets new standards in the quality of construction without significant cost premiums. In aggregate, the jury found the design to be instructive, aesthetically satisfying and technologically novel.

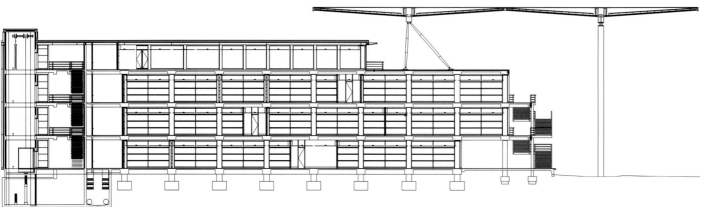

section

ground plan

Project Description

The University of Technology Petronas (UTP) campus is set in a dramatic landscape at Bandar Seri Iskandar, 300 kilometres north of Kuala Lumpur. Around two-thirds of the 450-hectare site is hilly and forested terrain, while the remainder is a plain dotted with dunes and man-made lakes formed by flooding disused mines.

The design responds both to the physical landscape and to the weather patterns in this part of the Malay Peninsula. It can be intensely hot in the sun, but during the monsoon season the skies open every afternoon to torrential rain. A soaring crescent-form roof covers the pedestrian routes that wind around the edge of the site, providing protection from the sun and rain while offering the comfort of cross-ventilating breezes. The steel columns that support the roof are slender, to maintain views, and from a distance the canopy elevation seems integrated with the tree canopy around the site.

To preserve the natural topography, the core academic buildings are laid out in a radial manner, skirting around the base of hills to form five 'crescents' that enclose a central landscaped park. These buildings are generally four storeys high and contain faculty offices, engineering laboratories, workshops and associated teaching facilities such as computer labs and tutorial spaces.

Tucked beneath the edges of the canopies, at four of the nodes where the crescents meet, are 'pocket buildings' containing lecture theatres, shops, cafes and student support facilities. At the fifth node, by the main entrance, is the social hub of the campus, the chancellor complex. This drum-like building, 21 metres high and around 150 metres in diameter, is formed of two crescent-shaped halves connected by a covered public plaza. One half of the building accommodates the resource centre with the library: the curve of the crescent is filled with four storeys of library stacks, visible through a vast glass and steel facade. The other half of the building houses the chancellor hall, a 3,000-seat auditorium with five tribunes, retractable seats and an excellent acoustic performance.

Given the acreage of the site, there would appear to be unlimited land on which to build. Yet for the campus to function well, the academic facilities had to be placed in close proximity to each other, especially in light of the varied topography and the warm climate. The distance a student can walk in the 10-minute break between classes – 800 metres – was used as the basic module of measurement for the pedestrian campus.

With a capacity of 6,600 students, UTP is the largest academic centre for the study of civil, mechanical, chemical and electrical engineering in the region. In terms of scale, the project is more consistent with town planning than with conventional building. The radial geometry of the scheme uses the topography of the site to locate five major axes along which the components of the university are organised. Several axes are kept open to provide the flexibility for long-term growth. Future phases of development include the completion of a sports stadium and a mosque (facilities that will be shared with the residents of a proposed new township) as well as additional student housing and research facilities.

The star configuration – a 'symbol of excellence' – originated in the very early stages of the planning for the university and was used as a template to zone various activities and initiate the preliminary design. When Foster + Partners and GDP took on the project they refined the concept. The masterplan was completed in March 2002. The challenge then was to deliver the project by August 2004.

Since the brief was to be developed in parallel with the design, the architects devised a loose-fit design strategy with generic laboratory types that would tolerate and accommodate more detailed functional requirements as they became known.

The construction technology in general took account of the capabilities of local contractors. The innovation lies in the rigour, detailing and quality of the work. The circular chancellor complex is formed using reinforced concrete slabs supported on steel columns. A double-curved steel structure roof clad in Kalzip covers its two halves. External elevations are curved pre-cast concrete with ceramic tiles, while internal elevations are glazing systems suspended by cables.

The academic buildings are predominantly flat-slab (pre-stressed) concrete, modularised bays supported by reinforced concrete columns. External elevations are modular single-skin glass panels organised in translucent and transparent finishes to respond to programme.

The roof canopy is insulated metal decking supported by tubular steel columns. The floor deck follows the roof plan, floating slightly above ground level with coloured pre-cast panels supported on steel frames.

Colour is used to blend the man-made with the natural; industrial methods with traditional materials. The local earth has a red hue that is replicated in finishes throughout the building. The exterior cladding is made of locally sourced ceramic tiles, on pre-cast panels, which form an iridescent pattern with varying matt and shiny finishes. In the chancellor complex, the interior cladding is mostly formed of silk panels that are woven to create rich patterns, using a traditional process integrating gold and silver threads.

Wherever possible the design has taken a holistic approach to using low-energy concepts. Whilst maintaining a harmony with the site, the blocks are separated by central passages that encourage airflow. The canopy acts as a very effective shading device for pedestrians and buildings alike. It is pierced with rooflights and edge louvres that allow daylight to filter through the interiors of the buildings. Cantilever passive shading and opaque glass reduce solar glare. Gas-fired centralised chilled water systems are used for cooling, and water is collected from the roof to be used for irrigation. Natural ventilation has been adopted wherever possible, for example in the support facilities and offices, but it is backed up by two types of mechanical ventilation.

The project has engendered an important transfer of knowledge, process, technology and confidence. The quality of the building reflects the fact that the designers were given the opportunity not only to conceive but also to deliver the project. Through working together, the two practices taught each other a lot about benchmarking, prototyping and meticulous detailing, and they are now collaborating on other projects. Similarly, the local contractors, who had not previously undertaken projects of this nature, have developed new skills and gone on to win new high-profile commissions in the region.

UTP provides a new 'prototype' of practice that links concept and expectation, creating an environment for an ambitious and progressive model of education.

Text adapted from a report
by Hanif Kara

roof plan

University of Technology Petronas
Bandar Seri Iskandar, Tronoh,
Malaysia

Client
Institute of Technology Petronas,
Malaysia

Architects
Foster + Partners, UK: Lord Norman
Foster, chairman; David Nelson,
head of design. GDP Architects Sdn
Bhd, Malaysia: Kamil Merican,
CEO and principal designer

Project Manager
KLCC Projects BHD, Malaysia

Engineers
Meinhardt Pte Ltd, Ranhill
Bersekutu Sdn Bhd, Wimsa HSS
Integrated and Majid & Associates
Sdn Bhd, structural engineers, all in
Malaysia; Roger Preston & Partners,
UK and Majutek Perunding,
Malaysia, mechanical engineers

Consultants
Research Facilities Design, USA,
landscape consultant; Sandy Brown
Associates, UK, acoustic consultant;
Marshall Day Acoustics, Malaysia,
acoustic consultants; BDG McColl,
Malaysia, signage; Jurukur Bahan
Malaysia/KPK, quantity surveyor;
Shah PK & Associates, Malaysia,
Gillespies, UK, landscape architects;
Lightsource International (Asia),
Hong Kong, lighting designer; PMP
Consultancy, UK, planner

Project Data
Built area: 104,000 m²
Site area: 85,000 m²
Cost: US$ 174,816,000
Commission: January 1998
Design: January 1998–January 2002
Construction: January 2002–
January 2004
Occupancy: August 2004

Websites
www.utp.edu.my
www.fosterandpartners.com
www.gdp.my

Foster + Partners was founded in
London in 1967 and is a worldwide
practice with project offices in more
than 20 countries. Over the past four
decades the company has been
responsible for a strikingly wide
range of work, from urban
masterplans, public infrastructure,
airports, civic and cultural buildings,
offices and workplaces to private
houses and product design. Norman
Foster, founder and chairman, was
born in Manchester in 1935. After
graduating from Manchester
University School of Architecture
and City Planning in 1961 he won a
Henry Fellowship to Yale University,
where he gained a Master's degree in
architecture. He became the 21st
Pritzker Architecture Prize Laureate
in 1999 and was awarded the
Praemium Imperiale Award for
Architecture in 2002.

David Nelson began working at
Foster's in 1976 and, since becoming
a partner in 1991, has worked on
many projects including Stanford
University Laboratories in California
and the new Supreme Court in
Singapore, in addition to the
University of Technology Petronas.
He was awarded an Honorary
Fellowship of the RIBA in 2002, and
now assumes a broader role within
the practice, sharing the overall
design direction as a lead member of
the design board. He became senior
executive head of design in 2007.

Group Design Partnership was
established in the year 1990. From
an initial staff of eight, it has grown
to become the largest architectural
practice in Malaysia, with a staff of
almost 250 people. In 1994, the firm
was incorporated as a private limited
company and has since come to be
known as GDP Architects Sdn Bhd or
simply GDP. Aside from architectural
services, GDP provides consultancy
services in numerous areas of design
and management such as masterplanning, interior design, graphic
design, feasibility studies and project
management. GDP take the stand that
design that addresses environment
and culture creates its own culture
and environment.

Kamil Merican is principal designer
and CEO of Group Design Partnership (GDP). He studied architecture
at Universiti Teknologi Malaysia
(UTM) and the Architectural
Association in London. He has
worked with various established
architectural firms including Farrell
and Grimshaw & Partners in
London and BEP Architects in
Malaysia. Merican has participated
in all manner of architectural and
masterplanning projects ranging
from commercial and corporate
buildings to institutional, hospitality
and industrial projects. He remains
actively involved with architectural
education and serves as a guest critic
at most universities in Malaysia. He
has been an external examiner for
UTM and Universiti Malaya (UM) for
over a decade.

Restoration of Amiriya Complex

Rada
Yemen

Selma Al-Radi
GOAMM
Yahya Al Nasiri

Introduction

The Amiriya was built at the beginning of the sixteenth century by the last ruler of Yemen's Tahirid dynasty, Amir Ibn 'Abd Al-Wahab. It consists of a highly ornamented and painted prayer hall, a *madrasa* and the private living quarters of the sultan. At the beginning of the 1980s the Amiriya was in a precarious condition. Any conventional restoration would have been a very costly undertaking, so the project director developed a well-defined philosophy to save the building which made pragmatic use of traditional methods of construction as well as local labour and materials. In this way, the restoration employed hundreds of local craftsmen and artisans, including in many cases several generations of the same family.

Jury Citation

The Amiriya, extraordinary in both its structure and its decoration, represents one of the richest and most complex Islamic styles found in the architecture of Yemen. Twenty-five years ago the building was in a state of extreme dilapidation; now it is completely restored through a remarkable project that has seen the recovery and revival of lost techniques of building and ornamentation, including the repair of elaborate carved stuccowork, the restoration of the rich tempera wall paintings, and a revival of the manufacture of *qudad*, the smooth waterproof plaster so prominent in Yemeni architecture. Over 500 craftsmen and artisans were trained during this project. Scores of them have since gone on to work on the restoration of many other buildings and monuments in the rest of Yemen (including one previous winner of the Aga Khan Award in 2004, the Al-Abbas Mosque). This effort has given an important impetus to the process of restoration and conservation in Yemen as a whole, which has innumerable major buildings in desperate need of rehabilitation.

The award has been given in recognition of the work of these craftsmen, and of the vision and persistence of those who have carried this project through to fruition.

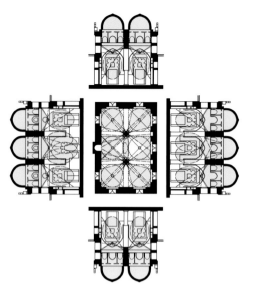

lighting system

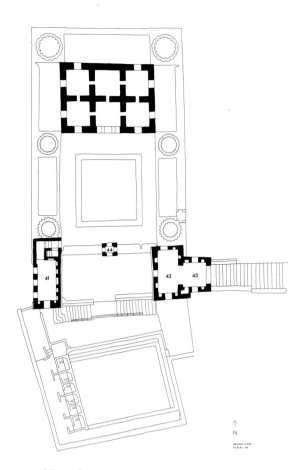

second floor plan

roofplan

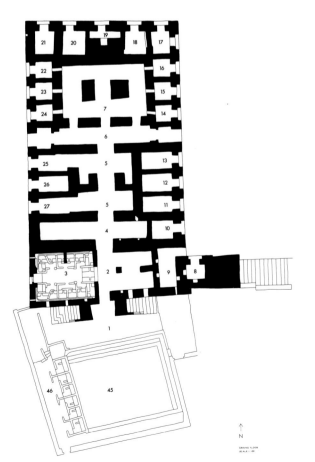

ground floor plan

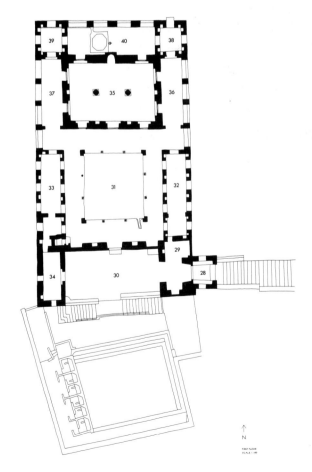

first floor plan

Project Description

Dressed all in white, the Amiriya glistens like a jewel – or an iced cake – in the stone and brick fabric of Rada. In this ornate building, the most ornate space is the *masjid* (prayer hall), which represents a highpoint of the type of decoration developed in the Tahirid period. Calligraphic bands of carved gypsum plaster run over openings and arches, delineating the structural elements as well as accentuating the importance of the spaces. A carved band also appears on the more important walls of the galleries. The *mihrab* and the intrados of domes and arches are decorated with other floral and geometric designs. The tempera paintings on the walls and domes of the prayer hall utilise a wide range of patterns, some of which show the influence of Indian textiles. *Qudad* plaster is used for waterproofing on the exterior, as well as decoratively in the geometric interlace on the south side of the east elevation, the panels on the sides of the stairs leading to the front courtyard, and the panels and individual figures around the platform beneath the *masjid* domes.

There is scant information on the use of the building until the twentieth century. Soon after the death of Sultan Amir the prayer hall was closed by Zaydi imams, who believed it to be overdecorated and distracting for worshippers. The Amiriya's funding from *waqf* sources was cut as well. The older sheikhs of Rada remember that the east rooms of the *madrasa* were used to chew *qat* in the afternoons, but the roof in this area caved in during the 1930s or 1940s. The school closed in the 1970s: some of its spaces were taken over by squatters while others were used for storage by shopkeepers.

By the 1980s the Amiriya was in very poor condition. Except on the west side, all the facades were sagging and bulging, with the walls cracked to varying degrees. Most of the flat ceilings had collapsed. The ground floor was badly treated by its users: some walls had been made thinner or taken down, and holes had been dug into the ground to create more storage space. The greatest damage was to the *qudad*, which had fallen off in places or cracked so that the building was no longer waterproof.

From the outset the project relied on the use of local labour and materials. Foreign expertise was required only in a few specialised areas, such as the restoration of the tempera paintings, which was undertaken by an Italian team from the Centro di Conservazione Archeologica (CCA) in Rome. The project received funding from the Yemeni, Dutch and, in the last phase, Italian governments.

One of the first actions was to consolidate the foundations. After this, under the supervision of master stonemason usta Izzi Muhammad Gas'a, the masonry walls were strengthened by a traditional technique known as *'scucio-cucio'* – 'unstitch-stitch'. This involves working in very small sections. One stone (or brick) is removed and the wall is supported by small props on the stones underneath. The infill and joints between are then filled if necessary and the stone is put back in place with new mortar. The central section of the north wall, however, had moved too far from the vertical to be restitched, and had to be taken down and reconstructed. A detailed survey of the facade formed the basis for a historically accurate reconstruction. As far as possible, the dismantled material was reused, though most bricks had to be replaced because they had lost their strength.

Much of what has been done at the Amiriya is the simple repair of elements that were either partly missing or in very bad condition. This of course took time, patience and the enduring skills of master masons and their team.

After the structure of the building was assured, the *qudad* on the roof and exterior of the building was replaced where necessary. Inside the prayer hall the old gypsum plaster was removed and a new layer applied. The window openings were fitted with sheets of alabaster. All repairs were made using the same materials and techniques as in the original structure. For example, when the *qudad* on the roof was replaced, it became apparent that very few of the beams had retained their supporting capacity, so new beams were made using the traditional timber, ilb.

The restoration project revived the production of certain materials and introduced new techniques for the use of others. *Qudad* is an ancient waterproof substance produced by mixing lime mortar with crushed volcanic aggregate. It was used for many centuries in Yemen but was abandoned after the introduction of cement. A few of the older masons working on the Amiriya vaguely remembered how to make it though they could not remember the exact ratio of ingredients, which was eventually found by trial and error. Some trials resulted in cracks that had to be repaired, but the long years of restoration also provided an opportunity for revising and perfecting the production and technique of application. Dr Al-Radi, the project director, published an article on the complete *qudad* experiment in 1987 in order to disseminate the information, and the material immediately began to be used in other restoration projects throughout the country.

The production of carved gypsum plaster was also revived. Dr Al-Radi herself started to clean away the many layers of whitewash that covered the carved decoration of the building, and trained many other people in this technique over the course of the restoration. The close contact with the material became a means to understand all the stages of its production, from beginning to end, as well as the technique of carving.

The restoration of the approximately 600 square metres of tempera wall paintings was simultaneously designed as an applied course to train Yemenis in the techniques of conservation. At the start of the project, the paintings were covered under a thick layer of dust, soot and whitewash, and had sustained damage as the building had become structurally unstable. After careful cleaning and consolidation, and some retouching with reversible materials and a final protective layer, the rich pigments and designs were once again exposed. The mural paintings are now beautifully illuminated through a clever lighting scheme with UV-free light fixtures suspended unobtrusively on four steel wires. The CCA has published a book about the conservation project as well as a report on the maintenance of the painted surfaces.

A museum on the Amiriya's ground floor tells the story of the monument's restoration, highlighting the achievements of Rada's builders past and present. However, the significance of the project goes far beyond the rehabilitation of an important monument. It represents a milestone in the protection of cultural heritage in Yemen, with its reliance on local knowledge and experience and revival of the country's historic architectural traditions.

Text adapted from reports by Ayşil Yavuz and Salma Samar Damluji

elevations

south

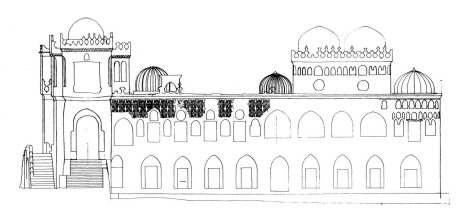

east

north

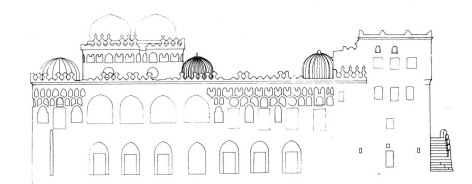

west

**Restoration of
Amiriya Complex**
Al Maydan, Rada, Yemen

Client
Government of Yemen, General
Organisation for Antiquities,
Museums and Manuscripts
(GOAMM): Yusuf Abdallah, director;
Qadi Ismail al Aqwa', director
(1983–1988)

Patron
Abdul Karim al-Iryani, former
Prime Minister of Yemen

Sponsor
Governments of Yemen,
The Netherlands and Italy

Project Directors
Selma Al-Radi, director
Yahya Muhammad Al-Nasiri,
director (1986–2005); Izzi
Muhammad Muslih, director
(1983–1986), GOAMM

Project Administration
American Institute for Yemeni Studies
(1994–2004): Christopher Edens,
resident director (2000–2004); Noha
Sadek (1996–1997), Marta Colburn
(1997–2000), former resident directors:
Koninklijk Instituut voor de Tropen
(KIT), Amsterdam (1983–1988)

GOAMM Staff
Adnan Jamil Nu'man, site manager;
Camillia Mohammad Ana'm, Abir
Atef Radwan, Jamal Mohammad
Thabet, Mohammad Abdel Wahab
No'uman, Rashad al Qubati, Adel
Said Mohammad, Ibrahim Ali Saad,
Saleh Naji Utaif, Amin Saleh Mauri,
team members

Craftsmen
usta Izzi Muhammad Gas'a, master
stone mason; usta Muhammad
Gas'a, usta Salih al-Basiri, usta
Abdul Rahman Lutfallah, master
builders; Mohammad Ali Sultan,
Abdallah Sultan, qudad masters;
Abd al Razzaq al-Usta, Qassim
Mohammad al-Usta, master
carpenters

**Conservation of
Mural Paintings**
Centro di Conservazione Archeo-
logica, Italy; Roberto Nardi, director;
Chiara Zizola, technical director

Stucco Restoration
Ali Hamud Abu al Futtuh al Nasiri,
Mohammad Hamud Abu al Futuh al
Nasiri, Mohammad Jarada

**Lighting and
Exhibition Design**
Architectenbureau Jowa,
Amsterdam, Jowa I. Kis-Jovak;
Erco Lighting, Germany, light
fixtures; Eyes on Media &
Vechtmetrieur, Amsterdam,
exhibition panels; Mohammad Abd
al-Wali, Yemen, electrical work

Project Data
Ground floor area: 920 m^2
Total floor area: 2,760 m^2
Cost: US$ 2,657,000
Commission: January 1983
Design: July 1983–January 2003
Construction: May 1986–
September 2005
Completed: September 2005

Bibliography
Selma Al-Radi, *The Amiriya in Rada*,
Oxford, 1997
Selma Al-Radi, Roberto Nardi and
Chiara Zizola, *Amiriya Madrasa:
The Conservation of the Mural
Paintings*, Rome, 2005

Selma Al-Radi is an Iraqi archaeo-
logist and a specialist on the medieval architecture of Yemen. She read
Oriental Studies at Cambridge
University and completed a PhD
at the Archaeological Institute,
University of Amsterdam. Dr Al-
Radi went to Yemen in 1977 to
catalogue the collection of the
National Museum in Sana'a and
restore the buildings to house the
museum. In 1983 she embarked
upon the restoration of the Amiriya
in Rada, a project that she steered
through to completion 25 years later.
Dr Al-Radi has excavated in Iraq,
Egypt, Kuwait, Cyprus, Syria and
Yemen, and has published extensively in Arabic and English.

Moulmein Rise Residential Tower

Singapore

WOHA Architects /
Wong Mun Summ
Richard Hassell

site plan

1 driveway
2 ramp to basement car park
3 guard house
4 roof of substation
5 generator (open to sky)
6 pool deck
7 lap pool
8 children's pool
9 landscape garden
10 metal pergola at roof top

ground plan

1 entrance forecourt
2 guard house
3 reflection pool
4 lobby
5 lift lobby
6 gymnasium
7 disabled shower
8 timber bridge
9 lap pool
10 children's pool
11 BBQ area

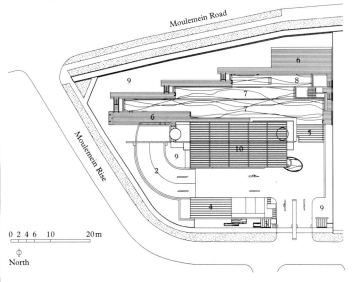

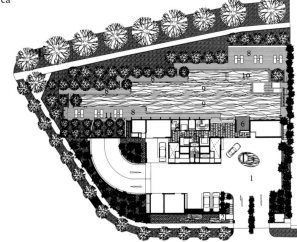

Introduction

This is a speculative residential high-rise in the tropics – with a difference. Instead of relying on mechanical systems for climate control, it borrows low-energy strategies from vernacular housing: orientation, internal planning, overhangs, cross-ventilation, shading and perforation are all reapplied here in a contemporary manner. And instead of treating the occupants as identical consumers, it allows for variation in both the plan and the facade, expressing individuality through recombining a small number of simple modular elements – much as DNA encodes diversity within a few simple proteins. Within the constraints of a developer-driven brief, the building establishes a distinctive urban presence – a refreshing change from the repetitive monotony of conventional stratified elevations – while providing privacy and comfort for the people who inhabit it.

Jury Citation

This building has received an award for its creative response to the issue of speculative high-rise housing, which avoids the kind of market-approved clichés that the client usually expects the architect to develop. In a field where attractive gestures on the facade tend to be valued more than spatial quality, the design offers an alternative that takes account of climate, spatial relations, site restrictions, daily living patterns and profit requirements. By transforming the various constraints into a set of didactic design guidelines, the architects were able to define a product that is quite different from the norm in the real-estate market.

The design addresses the challenges of the tropical climate by reinterpreting the traditional elements of the monsoon window and the perforated wall and by establishing a relation of different volumes to maximise air circulation. The facade ingeniously incorporates a version of the traditional balcony that responds to the needs of everyday life. The plans of the apartments are composed of basic geo-metric forms, enabling the client to maxi-mise sellable space while giving the users effective furnishing options. There is also an elegant use of materials and details. In all these respects, Moulmein Rise could be regarded more as a design approach than solely a built form.

elevations

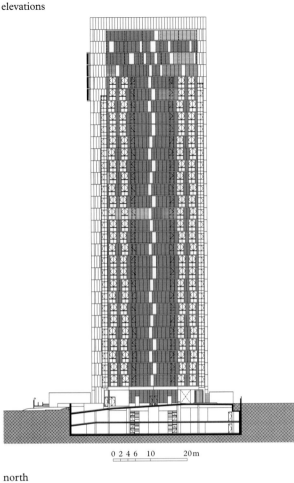

0 2 4 6 10   20m

north

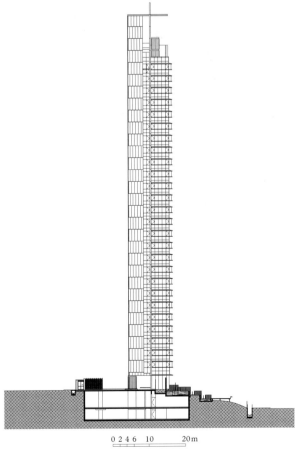

0 2 4 6 10   20m

east

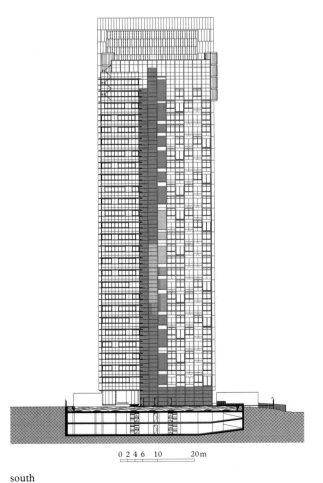

0 2 4 6 10   20m

south

0 2 4 6 10   20m

west

Project Description

No. 1 Moulmein Rise is a 28-storey building in a residential neighbourhood containing a mix of mid- to high-rises and single-family homes. Immediately to the south of the site is a conservation area where building heights are restricted to four storeys. Further south still there is a designated national park with a compound containing the president's residence. For security reasons, no building may face directly onto the compound; Moulmein Rise lies just outside this security zone. All of these factors work to the building's advantage, allowing it uninterrupted views of the surrounding open spaces and the downtown area beyond. The profusion of greenery creates a microclimate that is cooler than the city centre.

The building contains 48 typical apartments and two penthouse apartments. The ground floor has a gym as well as a 50-metre lap pool set in a tropical garden. The natural slope of the site was maintained by setting the pool over three cascading tiers. Underground parking is provided for 52 cars. There are two apartments per floor, and two private lifts that give direct access to each apartment; there is a separate public lift for visitors.

The original brief asked for a lower building with a deeper plan but the principal architects, Richard Hassell and Wong Mun Summ, persuaded the client to adopt a smaller footprint and go higher than he had intended. The resulting structure has a slender three-dimensional look that makes it stand out in Singapore's competitive real estate market. Its tallness produces added comfort for the occupants, improving cross-ventilation and increasing daylight into the building. With just two apartments per floor, there is also greater privacy.

In theory, Singapore high-rise dwellers benefit from the fresher air that circulates higher above the ground. In practice, few of them ever open their windows because of the unpredictability of the rain. This building incorporates monsoon windows – horizontal openings that let in the breeze but not the rain. The monsoon window is based on a traditional device used in the longhouses of Indonesia and here takes the form of a sliding aluminium panel incorporated into the bay window. The panel is operated by a winder, and a perforated metal shelf above the opening prevents objects from falling through. The device is well used, and many occupants sleep without air-conditioning.

The provision of natural means of climate control was of the utmost importance to the architects. The building is open on three sides and oriented north–south to optimise its environmental performance. The windows are well shaded to reduce direct heat into the apartments. Deep overhangs on the facades (1 metre on the north, and 0.6 metre with vertical sun screens on the south) provide shade and help keep out direct sunlight and driving rain.

The sometimes conflicting requirements of site, climate, technology, building regulations, developer, end users and consultants were all taken into account and incorporated into a set of strategic guidelines that were used to develop the design at all levels. A modular system based on multiples of 300 millimetres regulates all the architectural dimensioning, from floor-to-floor heights down to the smallest details.

The complex facade was created through the non-regular arrangement of standard elements. This principle of building up visual complexity was based on artist M.C. Escher's tessellations, which were inspired by the Islamic tiling of the Alhambra. Three different arrangements of planters, overhangs (horizontal sunshades), screens and monsoon windows were developed for the typical plan, stacked up in a random order. Three floor plate variations give strong variety to the facade.

In Singapore there is a huge demand for traditional features such as bay windows, sunshades and planters. The extra space they take up is exempt from development tax, but still counts as saleable area. Incorporating all these elements in a creative way added to the value of the apartments while simultaneously increasing their floor space by about 10 per cent. This conversion of commercial pressures into environmental devices is a key feature of the design.

The plan is simple, with the major spaces of living, dining and master bedroom to one side of the circulation spine, and the kitchen, two smaller bedrooms, washroom and utility to the other. Circulation or transitional space is defined by a different floor pattern and a lower ceiling. To accommodate changing user needs, the two smaller bedrooms have the potential to be combined into one. The open living area can also be adapted to a variety of functions.

Each apartment has three open sides, giving uninterrupted views of the surroundings – the open parkland and Singapore's downtown area beyond. This also creates the sense of a continuous flow of space, right from the entry to the far end of the apartment, usually a window in the master bedroom. The windows are operable and open inwards, making them easy to clean. (This was the first use of such windows in a Singapore high-rise in recent times.)

The building abounds with innovative details. A smart newspaper holder in the hallway doubles as a hook for umbrellas; curtain rods are concealed within the ceiling to give windows a crisp rectangular outline; sliding doors have custom-designed handles and locks that sit flush with the surface; unobtrusive door frames were specially designed to maintain the planar effect of the doors; and air-conditioning is concealed inside the low ceiling of the circulation spine.

The choice of materials was determined by issues of economy, durability, availability and aesthetics. Exposed concrete surfaces are finished with a proprietary textured coating in colours selected to mask dirt or construction tolerances. The environmentally responsive curtain wall incorporates tempered glass, aluminium, wood, steel and timber-clad steel.

The front or south facade presents an elegant play of shadow and shifting screens, while the back facade takes the form of a vast service cage concealing the air-conditioning units, drying racks and other utilities that so often mar the appearance of high-rise buildings. The tall blade wall that rises from the top of the roof dramatically expresses the division between major and minor spaces in the apartments.

Moulmein Rise has the presence of a coherent urban object that reflects the viability of the plan that it holds. There is an integral relationship between its external form and internal arrangements. It takes advantage of the incentives offered by Singapore planning regulations by adopting traditional features that contribute to climate control, but incorporates them in new ways. Innovative, yet at the same time entirely practical, it offers a humane, imaginative response to a standard developer brief.

Text adapted from a report by Zainab Faruqui Ali

typical floor layout

1 fire lift lobby
2 private lift lobby
3 living/dining
4 kitchen
5 yard
6 utility
7 master bedroom
8 bedroom 2
9 bedroom 3

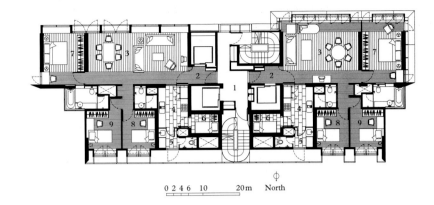

0 2 4 6 10   20m   North

upper penthouse layout

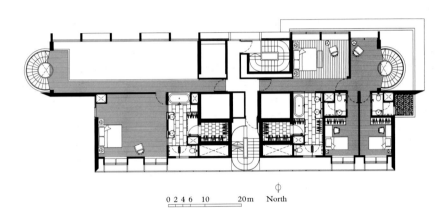

0 2 4 6 10   20m   North

typical facade details at east apartments

typical facade details at west apartments

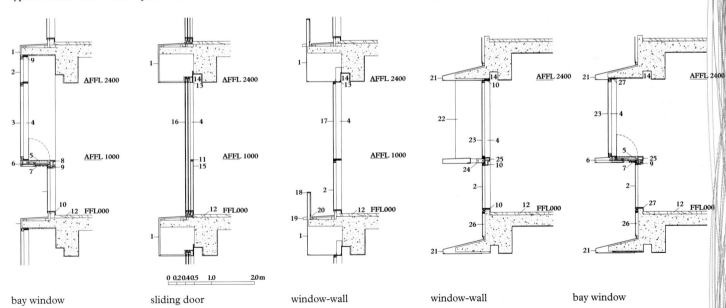

0 0.20.40.5 1.0   2.0 m

bay window   sliding door   window-wall   window-wall   bay window

1 alucobond sheet for ledge
2 fixed tempered glass
3 open-in casement window
4 steel mullion
5 perforated aluminium fixed to hinged frame
   with insect screen between (closed position)
6 mdf board sliding (closed position)
7 safety bars
8 'l' steel bracket
9 handle winder

10 timber lining
11 timber handrail
12 parquet flooring with marine ply underlay
13 veneered ply
14 curtain recess
15 steel balustrades
16 sliding tempered glass door
17 open-out casement
18 end fixing plate
19 water outlets

20 aluminium gutter
21 alucobond sheet for hood
22 alucobond linding
23 open-out casement sash for ventilation
    and cleaning
24 aluminium outrigger plates at mullion centres
25 rhs bracket
26 ventilated cavity
27 ash veneer ply with edge veneer

Moulmein Rise Residential Tower
No. 1 Moulmein Rise, Singapore

Client
UOL Development Pte Ltd,
Singapore

Architects
WOHA Architects, Singapore:
Wong Mun Summ, Richard Hassell,
partners

Contractors
Shining Construction Pte Ltd,
Singapore; Arzbergh Engineering
Group Pte Ltd, Singapore; Fairways
Construction & Landscapes Pte Ltd,
Singapore; Hitachi Asia Ltd.,
Singapore; Sum Cheong Piling Pte
Ltd, Singapore; Venus Enterprises
Pte Ltd, Singapore; Focchi Pte Ltd,
Singapore; Magnificent Seven
Corporation Pte Ltd, Singapore

Engineers
Meinhardt Pte Ltd, Singapore,
mechanical engineer; Dai-Dan Co.
Ltd, Singapore, electrical engineer;
Acacia Engineering Pte Ltd,
Singapore, plumbing

Consultants
KPK Quantity Surveyors (1995)
Singapore Pte Ltd, quantity
surveyor; ABL Lim (FPC) Pte Ltd,
Singapore, fire safety; Shin Nippon
Air Technologies Co Ltd, Singapore,
air conditioning consultants

Project Data
Ground floor area: 230 m²
Built area: 6,491 m²
Site area: 2,340 m²
Cost: US$ 9,137,000
Commission: November 1999
Design: November 1999–April 2001
Construction: April 2001–May 2003
Completed: May 2003

Bibliography
'Monsoon Cool', *Architectural
Review*, December 2004
'High, Medium, Low', *Architecture
Asia 3*, 2004
*New Directions in Tropical Asian
Architecture*, WOHA Periplus
Publishing 2005
10 x 10_2: 100 Architects, 10 Critics,
Phaidon 2005
'Asian Breezes: Towards Sustainable
Architecture, No. 1 Moulmein Rise',
JIA, 2005
'Svelte Suburban' *Architecture +
Design 10*, 2004
'Size Does Not Matter', *Singapore
Architect*, June 2005

Website
www.wohadesigns.com

Formed in 1994 by Singaporean
Wong Mun Summ and Australian
Richard Hassell, WOHA brings
together a mix of designers from
diverse backgrounds to explore
integrated design for the built
environment, encompassing
masterplanning, architecture,
landscape, interiors, lighting and
furniture design. WOHA has received
numerous international awards for
excellence in design, and has been
published extensively. It has offices
in Singapore and Thailand, and has
been involved in projects all around
the Asia Pacific region.

Wong Mun Summ graduated with
honours from the National
University of Singapore in 1989.
Before establishing his private
practice in July 1994, he worked in
the office of Kerry Hill Architects on
projects around Southeast Asia,
including the acclaimed Datai Resort
in Langkawi, Malaysia. He has
received numerous design awards
including the Royal Australian
Institute of Architects International
Award in 1999 and the Singapore
Institute of Architects Award in
2001, 2003 and 2004.

Richard Hassell received a bachelor
of architecture degree with first class
honours from the University of
Western Australia, Perth, in 1989
and a master's degree in architecture
from the Royal Melbourne Institute
of Technology in 2002. He has been
a member of the Design Singapore
Council since 2005 and has taught at
the University of Technology,
Sydney, Australia and the University
of Hawaii at Manoa.

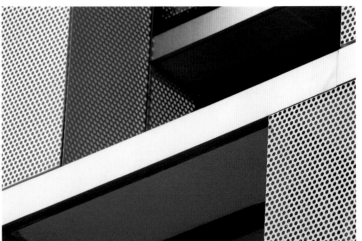

Royal Netherlands Embassy

Addis Ababa
Ethiopia

Dick van Gameren and
Bjarne Mastenbroek

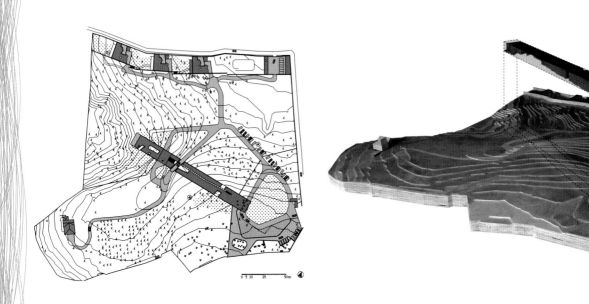

0 5 10   25   50m

Introduction

The embassy complex lies on the southern outskirts of Addis Ababa, in a dense eucalyptus grove set amidst urban sprawl. The main building, an elongated horizontal volume, cuts across the sloping terrain on an east-west axis. Around one third of the way down its length, a driveway passes through it at first-floor level, separating the ambassador's residence from the chancellery. The flat roof that unites the two parts is a roof garden accessed from elevated pathways.

Inside the chancellery, offices flank a ramped corridor that climbs the gradient of the site, ending in a patio linked to the roof. Walls, floors and ceilings are pigmented the same red-ochre as the Ethiopian earth and are uniformly composed of concrete, creating the effect of a cave-like space. By contrast the roof garden, with its network of shallow pools, alludes to a Dutch water landscape. Other contemporary Dutch themes are expressed in the building's programmatic diversity, its crisp transparencies and its oversailing cantilevers.

Jury Citation

An unashamedly contemporary and simple organisation of spaces, the Dutch Embassy in Addis Ababa overcomes the complexities of security and surveillance normally associated with the design of embassy compounds, intersecting with the landscape to create new and unexpected relationships with the host site – a walled eucalyptus grove in the city. The massif architecture, at once archaic and modern, belongs as much to the Muslim, Christian and indigenous peoples of Ethiopia as it does to its Dutch homeland.

In its conception and daily operation, the building responds to its social and physical context with inventive design and poetic sensibility. This is an architecture that works with its environment, reducing the use of mechanical services and relying instead on natural ventilation and high insulation. The project's sensitivity to process has left its mark in the raw character of its formation – another delicate reminder of how buildings, as formations of material culture, can register and enhance spaces of encounter.

roof detail

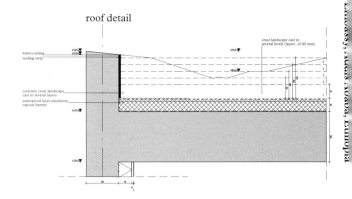

horizontal detail and front view
window type CR-A

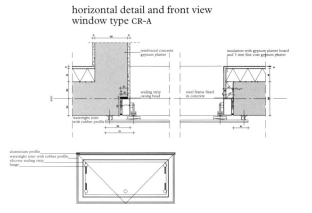

vertical detail
principal detail window type CR-A

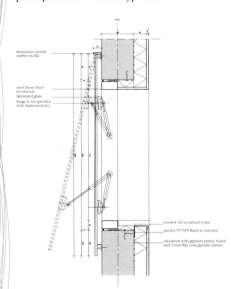

vertical detail
room number: R.007

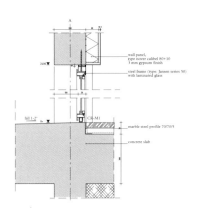

vertical detail
room number: R.1.07/R.0.08

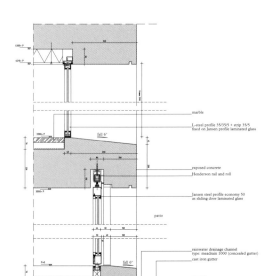

south elevation

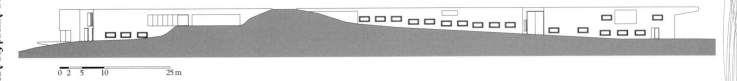

0 2 5 10   25 m

cross sections

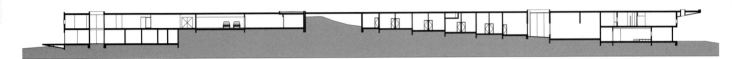

roof landscape

upper level of chancellery and residence

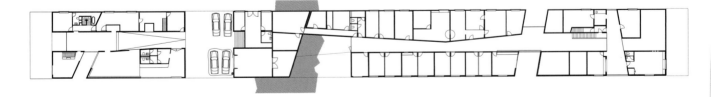

lower level of chancellery and residence

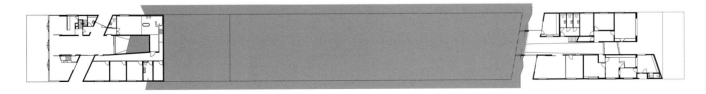

Project Description

The project was commissioned in 1998 by the Dutch Ministry of Foreign Affairs as part of a programme to construct new embassy buildings that would represent contemporary Dutch culture and at the same time respect the local environment and create meaningful collaborations with local professionals and firms. The diplomatic compound had been in use since the 1940s, but the existing chancellery was housed in a temporary building while the ambassador's residence was in a dilapidated old villa. The brief called for the construction of a new chancellery, ambassador's residence and three staff houses, as well as the refurbishment and expansion of the old villa to accommodate the deputy ambassador. A small school building and gatehouse were later added to the programme.

Two other embassies – those of Saudi Arabia and Cameroon – are located to the south of the five-hectare site. The rest of the neighbourhood is characterised by a mix of undistinguished low-cost housing, small shops and a ring road. In this context, the compound is a small oasis of greenery. The architects' guiding principle was to preserve this quality, minimising the impact of the new construction. Existing contour lines were maintained, and care was taken not to disturb the vegetation or wildlife. The arrangement of the individual programme elements is designed to create maximum privacy, as if each building stood alone in this beautiful natural setting.

The gatehouse signals the embassy's presence from the busy ring road. As a gesture of transparency and accessibility, a perforated panel gives a view of the main building's projecting roof even before the moment of entry. A winding driveway leads through the lavish greenery, with a series of views of the building unfolding along the way. The road then intersects the building, passing underneath its roof to connect with the deputy ambassador's house at the western end of the site.

The northern boundary of the site is marked by the small school building and three staff houses, placed one behind the other as on a terrace, so the occupants can enjoy unobstructed views from their elevated position.

The main building's horizontal mass measures 140 x 15 metres and sits on a ridge of sloping ground, cutting into the topography at this ridgeline and adapting its base to the rest. The driveway that passes through the building divides it into two, with the ambassador's residence in the smaller western portion and the chancellery in the east. The roof garden, with its contoured, landscaped surface covered with a series of pools, unites the two parts. At its eastern extremity, the roof juts out to form

a daring 11-metre canopy that defines the public face of the building, the point of arrival and entry.

The eastern third of the chancellery is two storeys high; the ambassador's offices are upstairs, with views over both the outside porch and the long internal corridor. The offices are linked to the residence by a rooftop path. On the ground floor, a ramped corridor flanked by offices gently climbs the gradient of the site, from the entry hall to the far end of the building. The course of this corridor changes twice, first enlarging to become a small foyer with a patio on two sides, then deviating slightly towards the middle to accommodate the swelling of office sizes on one side. It terminates in a sloped patio that in turn connects to the roof.

The two-storey residence at the western end of the building has a tripartite layout with internalised core spaces – the private quarters of the ambassador at the lower level and formal reception spaces above. As the building conforms to the sloping terrain, both levels can be entered from various points outside. A sloped patio at the formal entrance to the residence links the two floors, and a flight of stairs leads from the patio to the roof. The floors are connected internally by three concealed staircases.

Daylight is funnelled into these spaces through the sloped patio, which is cut deeply into the building. There are a number of further incisions along the length of the block, which draw indirect northern and southern light through their transparent edges. Apart from these incisions and the restrained fenestration, the building mass is almost monolithic. The red-ochre walls (pigmented with ferrous oxide) have a rough texture created by misalignments in the concrete formwork, making it seem as if the structure has been carved out of the ground.

The architects have said that the formal vocabulary of the design stems from an encounter of traditional Ethiopian architecture with Dutch cultural and architectural themes, with the aim of inspiring 'an exchange of ideas between two worlds, Europe and Africa'. The primary cultural reference is the rock-hewn architecture of the Coptic churches in Lalibela, which are dug down to a depth of two to three storeys, interconnecting with the landscape, then vanishing into it.

The second major cultural reference comes from the architects' homeland. The sculptural rivulets of the 'roof/pool' allude to the Dutch way of managing water and the polder landscape. During the rainy season the roof becomes a shallow pool. At other times it resembles a dried-up riverbed.

The main building's structure is a reinforced concrete flat slab and shear wall system, unencumbered by columns or beams. It is structurally divided into four

parts, with three expansion joints. The concrete technology is straightforward, almost conventional, except for the entrance cantilever.

All the concrete was poured in place, using a handmade formwork in natural wood. To give the material an individual touch, each of the 14- or 15-centimetre planks was slightly tilted to make recesses and projections and create a striated texture, which is accentuated under the play of sunlight. No standardised measure was specified for this purpose; the planks were misaligned using a stick or by hand.

The embassy building's interior design is a direct outcome of its architecture, constituting a plain backdrop for the artworks and artefacts on display; it is the minimalist surfaces alone that create an architecture of planes, both solid and transparent.

The building has no mechanical heating, ventilation or air-conditioning system, except in the reception spaces of the ambassador's residence where there is a limited HVAC system (used only for ventilation, to minimise energy consumption). Environmental control issues are generally solved in a natural way, mainly through the insulating properties of the earth and the added layers of insulation in the walls, ceilings and floors. Chimneys are provided in every space, some with fireplaces, in case the need arises for additional heating.

This sensitivity to place is also reflected in the project's engagement with the local workforce and building industry. The project was built by local contractors using the predominant local construction material – concrete.

The embassy complex took eight years to realise. The delay between the start of the design, in May 1998, and the start of construction, in December 2002, was necessary for the two sides to become familiar with each other's way of working and for Dutch procedures of tendering to be adapted to local ones.

Text updated from a report by Aydan Balamir

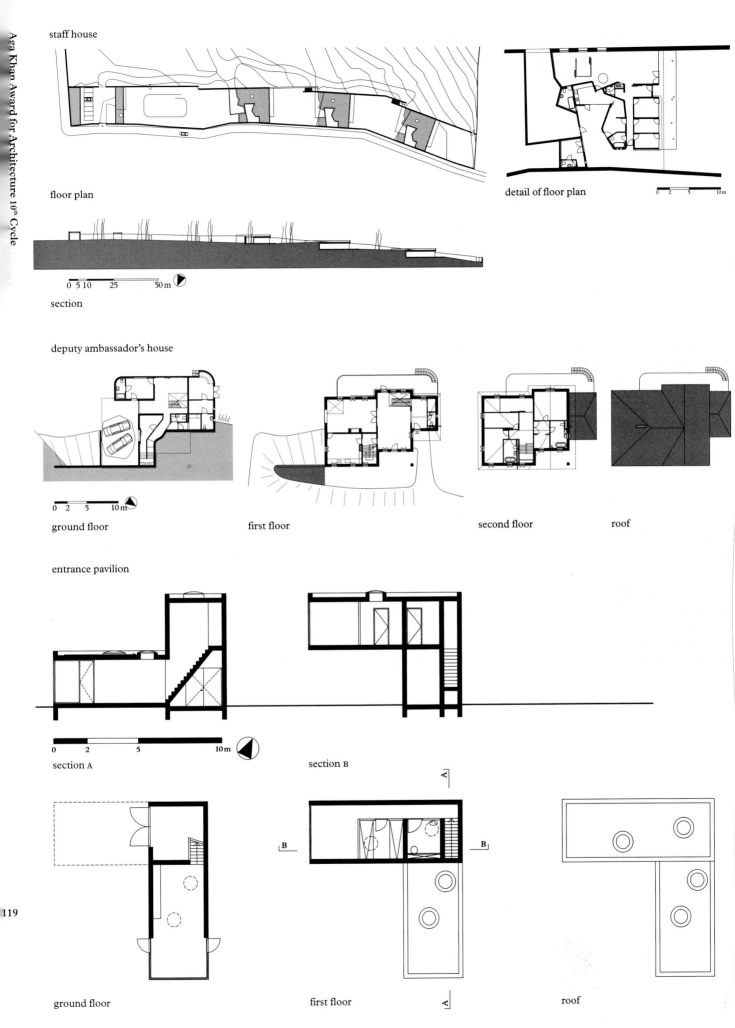

staff house

floor plan

detail of floor plan

0 2   5   10 m

0 5 10   25   50 m

section

deputy ambassador's house

0 2   5   10 m

ground floor

first floor

second floor

roof

entrance pavilion

section A

section B

0   2   5   10 m

A

B   B

A

ground floor

first floor

roof

Royal Netherlands Embassy
Old Airport Zone W24, K13,
House 001, Addis Ababa, Ethiopia

Client
Dutch Ministry of Foreign Affairs,
The Netherlands

Architects
Dick van Gameren and Bjarne
Mastenbroek, The Netherlands;
ABBA Architects, Ethiopia: Rahel
Shawl, local architect

Local Project Manager
Gary Campbell, Ethiopia

Engineers
Arup Associates, engineering
consultant, UK; Campbell Manage-
ment Project Services: Yared
Belayneh, resident engineer; San-
Mech Consult: Worede Melaku, local
sanitary and mechanical engineer;
FASTEK Consult: Fessahaie Kelati,
electrical engineering consultant;
OTT Consulting Architects &
Engineers: Mr. Mesfin Bereded,
resident architect

Contractor
Elmi Olindo & Co Plc, Ethiopia

Project Data
Built area: 3,300 m²
Site area: 55,000 m²
Cost: US$ 7,332,000
Commission: May 1998
Design: May 1998–May 2002
Construction: December 2002–
April 2006
Occupancy: June 2005

Bibliography
Catherine Slessor, 'Dutch Embassy,
Addis Ababa, Ethiopia', *Architectural
Review*, May 2006
Chiara Baglione, 'Ambasciata dei
Paesi Bassi, Addis Abeba, Ethiopia',
Casabella, April 2006
'Dutch Embassy in Ethiopia, *Detail*,
January/February 2006

Websites
www.netherlandsembassyethiopia.org
www.dickvangameren.nl
www.search.nl

Dick van Gameren (b. 1962)
graduated from Delft University of
Technology in 1988. He founded an
office with Bjarne Mastenbroek in
1991, and two years later they joined
the architectengroep in Amsterdam.
He now runs his own office, Dick
van Gameren Architecten BV. His
work has won several prizes and been
the subject of monographs published
by 010 in 2001 and NAi in 2005. He
was appointed Professor of
Architectural Design at Delft University of Technology in 2005.

Bjarne Mastenbroek (b. 1964)
studied in Delft and worked first for
Mecanoo in Delft and then for Enric
Miralles in Barcelona. In 1991 he
founded an office with Dick van
Gameren; in 1993 they became part
of the architectengroep in Amsterdam. In 2002, with Ad Bogerman, he
established SeARCH, which brings
together 30 international architects
and designers. SeARCH develops
architectural and urban projects and
undertakes research on architecture,
landscaping, urbanism and new
building products and materials.

Rehabilitation of the Walled City

Nicosia
Cyprus

Nicosia Master
Plan Team

buffer zone

Introduction

Nicosia's rich and sometimes turbulent past is reflected in its urban and architectural composition, most markedly in its historic walled core. The city experienced centuries of foreign rule – Ptolemaic, Roman, Byzantine, Crusader/Lusignan, Venetian, Ottoman and British – before becoming the capital of an independent Cyprus in 1960. In 1974 the city was violently split into two sectors, separated by a buffer zone.

Since 1979, a remarkable effort has been made to regenerate the walled city and protect its architectural and urban heritage. What makes this initiative unique is the fact that it has been carried out on the local level by both the Turkish Cypriot and Greek Cypriot communities of the city. This was the first (and for some time the only) joint project carried out by the two communities and it has been a sustained effort, uninterrupted by the ebb and flow of politics. The most peculiar aspect is that there is no written agreement on this matter between the communities, only scattered notes relating to project works.

Jury Citation

The representatives of the Greek Cypriot and Turkish Cypriot communities of Nicosia decided to transcend a tense political situation and take the first steps towards reversing the city's physical decay and economic decline through the catalyst of restoring the historic walled city. Out of this initiative grew a rehabilitation programme that would ultimately enhance the wellbeing of all the inhabitants of Nicosia.

The project has maintained a high standard of workmanship and skills in urban restoration and renewal and involved close cooperation between Greek Cypriot and Turkish Cypriot members of the project team. The preservation of the cultural and architectural legacy of the historic centre has provided an impetus for private investment, attracted new residents, encouraged tourism and strengthened economic activity. In addition, the rehabilitated buildings are breathing life into the divided city, and new cafés, restaurants, cultural centres and public spaces abound.

The project is a fine example of how, with tolerance and sensitivity, opposing sides can be brought together to build a shared space for all people and all faiths.

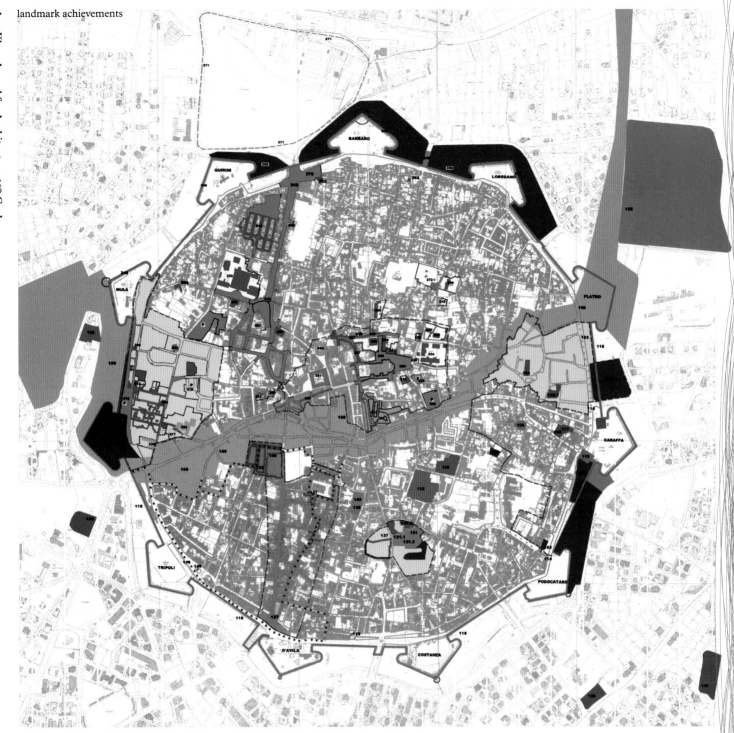

rehabilitation projects
restoration of monuments
restoration of listed buildings
public intensive uses
pedestrianisation-infrastructure
landscaping
survey and documentation
--- improvement of traffic circulation
partial restoration/facades
--- project area

walking tour: Nicosia
... walking tour: Medieval Nicosia
... walking tour: Revitalisation of Nicosia

Project Description

The present city wall – which replaced earlier medieval fortifications – was built by the Venetians between 1567 and 1570. It was intended to repel an anticipated Ottoman invasion, but the Ottomans still managed to capture the city less than a year after its completion. The wall has a very distinctive geometric outline, forming a circle with eleven spearhead bastions spaced equally along its perimeter. There are three historic gates, to the north, east and west, along with further entry points for motor vehicles that were added during the modern period.

The walled city has a diameter of about 1.6 kilometres and covers an area of about 2 square kilometres. Its buildings are constructed of a soft, yellowish stone and rendered sun-dried brick in a variety of styles that mirror the city's diverse history – Byzantine, Gothic and Ottoman – as well as more recent vocabularies ranging from neo-classical to modernist.

Like most cities, Nicosia has been changed by the forces of modernisation. Beginning in the period of British rule and reaching a climax in the 1960s, its tightly knit urban fabric was undermined as streets were widened to accommodate traffic, and old buildings torn down to make way for new developments. A notorious example of this was the demolition in 1931 of sections of the wall on both sides of the historic Kyrenia Gate to ease traffic flow through the city. Nonetheless, the damage caused by such interventions remains limited in comparison to many other cities.

Much more detrimental was the imposition, in 1974, of a buffer zone passing right through the heart of the walled city. What was once a central and commercially vibrant quarter became, at a stroke, an uninhabited no-man's-land patrolled by United Nations peace-keepers. The adjacent areas to the north and south also deteriorated as the organic links between neighbourhoods were abruptly severed.

In 1979 the representatives of the two communities of Nicosia, Mustafa Akıncı and Lellos Demetriades, held a historic meeting under United Nations auspices and agreed to work together on problems affecting the city. They reached an agreement of cooperation at a time when other forms of collaboration between the two sides were non-existent. The first issue they addressed was the completion of a unified sewage system for the city. A year later they launched the comprehensive Nicosia Master Plan (NMP) project, which treats the city as a united entity.

The rehabilitation of the old city was from the outset an important component of the master plan. Surveys, studies and plans for the historic centre were drawn up, with every effort made to involve the two communities equally, and to bring together a dedicated team of architects and planners from both the Turkish Cypriot and Greek Cypriot sides. A joint team of architects executed a detailed survey of all the buildings of the buffer zone before rehabilitation work began.

The first implementation phase started in 1986. This included twin projects for the rehabilitation of two areas located along the buffer zone: Arab Ahmet in the northern part of the city and Chrysaliniotissa in the south. The process of surveying buildings of historical and architectural importance was begun, resulting in the listing of about 1,100 buildings in the south and 630 in the north. (Before 1986, only the main monuments were listed.) A legal framework was developed to ensure the enforcement of the protection, including development transfer rights and height restrictions set at two storeys.

Restoration activity since the late 1980s has encompassed the eighteenth-century aqueduct, the north facade of Omeriye Mosque (originally the Latin Church of St Mary of the Augustinians) and the Tahtakale Mosque. Efforts have been made to pedestrianise commercial areas such as Ledras and Onasagorou Streets, Kyrenia Avenue and Arasta Street. Public open spaces have been improved, with the construction of Chrysaliniotissa Garden, the redesign of Phaneromeni Square, the paving of Selimye Square and the creation of an open space between the Omeriye monument and baths.

The built environment of urban neighbourhoods has been significantly improved by the restoration of facades and the upgrading of infrastructures, including roads. Specific projects have dealt with the neighbourhoods of Phaneromeni, Arch. Philotheou Street, Samanbahçe and Selimiye.

Wherever possible, restorations have incorporated traditional materials and techniques, and all interventions are designed to be reversible. But this is not a process of 'museumification': a number of adaptive re-use projects have a strong contemporary feel – as can be seen in the conversion of the 1930s power station into a modern art gallery. Many other historically significant structures have also been restored to serve new functions: a traditional building in the Arab Ahmet area is now a culture and arts centre; another restored traditional house is being used as a kindergarten in Chrysaliniotissa; the Buyuk Khan (Great Inn) has been transformed into a multipurpose centre with antiques shops, art galleries and a cafeteria; and the old Dervis Pasha and Eaved House mansions are now museums.

Other projects have returned buildings to their original functions. The sixteenth-century Omeriye baths are once again open to the public, as is the old municipal market. The 'Fourni' (traditional oven) building has been restored and is being reused as a laboratory for the study of traditional building materials and techniques.

After two decades and the implementation of dozens of projects, the historic centre has reasserted its role in contemporary Nicosia. The rehabilitated core offers not only a rich architectural heritage but also a healthy urban environment where all services are within walking distance, where pedestrian movement takes priority over motor traffic, and where significant economic opportunities are evolving. The infrastructure is being comprehensively upgraded, from the level of the street paving to the renewal of the water, electricity, sewage and telecommunications networks. In some instances, such as the Chrysaliniotissa project, a policy of offering subsidised housing to young families has injected new life into neighbourhoods with elderly populations (and in the process helped the long-term residents feel part of a vibrant community again). The large-scale projects have also triggered the restoration of numerous private houses, with grants available to cover up to 40 per cent of the cost of the work.

Beyond their impact on the built fabric, the restoration activities of the NMP have had a most interesting effect on the cultural life of Nicosia: there are now numerous joint cultural activities between the Turkish Cypriot and Greek Cypriot communities, from photo exhibitions to theatre performances and folk dances.

A bold and forward-thinking project, the Nicosia Master Plan has brought together opposing communities by identifying what unites rather than divides them. It has used the shared space of a historic urban core as the motor to develop a relationship of cooperation and positive coexistence that has continued to evolve over a quarter of a century.

Text adapted from a report by Mohammad al-Asad

repair and reinforcement

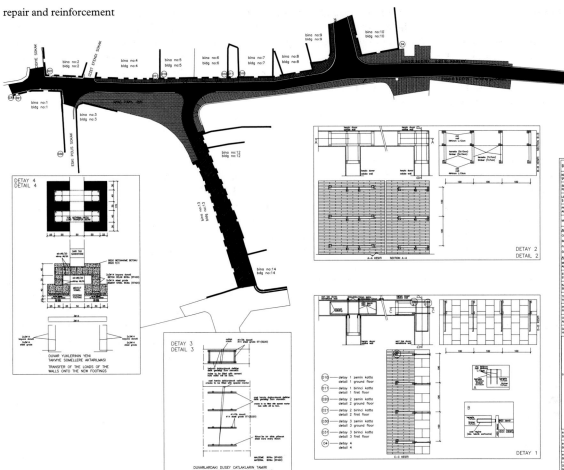

elevations

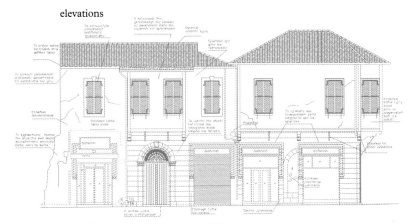

Ledra Street, west – existing condition

Pigmalion Street, east – existing
condition (left) and proposal (right)

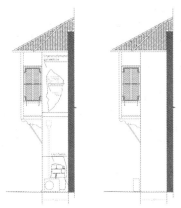

Ledra Street, west – proposal

Rehabilitation of the Walled City
Nicosia, Cyprus

Client
Greek Cypriot and Turkish Cypriot
Communities of Nicosia

Initiators
Lellos Demetriades, Representative
to the NMP (1979–2000)
Mustafa Akıncı, Representative to
the NMP (1979–1990)

Current Representatives
Eleni Mavrou, Representative of the
Greek Cypriot community
Cemal Bulutoğuları, Representative
of the Turkish Cypriot community

Coordinators
United Nations Development
Programme (UNDP)
United Nations High Commission
for Refugees (UNHCR)

Sponsors
United States Agency for
International Development (USAID)
and the European Union

Nicosia Master Plan Teams
Greek Cypriot community: Agni
Petridou, team leader; Athina
Papadopoulou, Elena Sofianou,
Eleni Petropoulou, Nayia Savvides,
Marina Tymviou, Simos Droussiodes,
George Tsangarides, architects; Paris
Skouloukos, civil engineer; George
Passiardis, quantity surveyor; Elena
Papamichael, Iro Ioannou, junior
architects; Yianna Constantinou, Poli
Votsi, Andreas Giallouros, Demoulla
Metaxa, Frosso Anastasiou, techni-
cians; Christos Kyriakou, Caterina
Photiou, office assistants, all in Cyprus

Turkish Cypriot Community:
Ali Güralp, team leader; Cemal
Bensel, Ali Kodan , Gamze
Keleşzade, architects; Zeka Yılmaz,
Hüseyin Cakır, civil engineers: Ayça
S. Cıralı, town planner; Mustafa
Kelebek, technician; Gül Öztek,
Hülya Davulcu, Emine Pilli, Ahmet
Buçaner, Kerime Darbaz, Aydın
Tayyareci, Mehmet Kanan, team
members, all in Cyprus

Project Data
Site area: 2,010.000 m²
Cost: US$ 18,749,000 (Greek Cypriot
side) 1986–2007
Cost: US$ 6,900,000 (Turkish
Cypriot side) 1986–2007
Commission: 1979
Planning: 1981
Design: 1986 ongoing
Construction: 1987 ongoing
Occupancy: 1989 ongoing

Bibliography
*Nicosia Master Plan, Walled Nicosia:
A Guide to its Historical and Cultural
Sites* (Nicosia: NMP, n.d.)
United Nations Development
Programme, *Revitalizing Old Nicosia*
(Nicosia: n.d.)

Websites
www.undp-unops.org
www.nicosia.org.cy
www.undp-act.org

In 1979, at a meeting of the
representatives of both the Greek
Cypriot and Turkish Cypriot
communities in Nicosia, it was
agreed that the two sides should co-
operate closely for the purpose of
preparing a common masterplan for
the proper unified development of
the city. The objective of the project
was the improvement of the built
environment and living conditions
of all the inhabitants of the city.

A bi-communal, multidisciplinary
team of national and international
experts was formed in 1981 to
prepare a joint master plan for
Nicosia. The team consists of town
planners, architects, civil engineers,
sociologists, economists and experts
in traffic and transportation,
conservation, landscape, urban
finance as well as other technical
staff. The formation of this team was
one of the first attempts at technical
cooperation between the two
communities.

Initial funding for the Nicosia
Master Plan (NMP) project was
provided by the United States
Agency for International Deve-
lopment (USAID). Implementation
was carried out through the United
Nations High Commission for
Refugees (UNHCR), the United
Nations Development Programme
(UNDP) and the United Nations
Office for Project Services (UNOPS).
More recently, funding has also been
provided by the European Union.

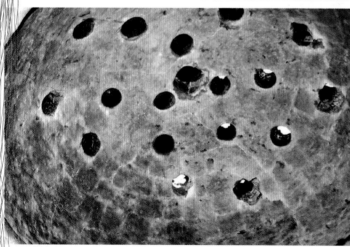

School in Rudrapur

Dinajpur
Bangladesh

Anna Heringer and
Eike Roswag

Introduction

This school was hand-built in four months by local craftsmen, pupils, parents and teachers together with experts and volunteers from Germany and Austria. It is located in the compound of a Bangladeshi NGO, Dipshikha, which is dedicated to integrated and sustainable rural development. The philosophy of the school's educational programme is 'learning with joy', with an emphasis on helping the children to develop their own potential and use it in a creative way. The building follows the same principles, bringing out the best in local materials by inventively combining them with improved construction techniques. The lower portion consists of rammed straw-reinforced mud walls finished with battered mud; the upper floor is a bamboo frame construction with slatted bamboo for the walls, windows and doors; the roof is finished with sheets of corrugated galvanised iron.

Jury Citation

This joyous and elegant two-storey primary school in rural Bangladesh has emerged from a deep understanding of local materials and a heart-felt connection to the local community. Its innovation lies in the adaptation of traditional methods and materials of construction to create light-filled celebratory spaces as well as informal spaces for children. Earthbound materials such as loam and straw are combined with lighter elements like bamboo sticks and nylon lashing to shape a built form that addresses sustainability in construction in an exemplary manner.

The design solution may not be replicable in other parts of the Islamic world, as local conditions vary, but the approach – which allows new design solutions to emerge from an in-depth knowledge of the local context and ways of building – clearly provides a fresh and hopeful model for sustainable building globally. The final result of this heroic volunteer effort is a building that creates beautiful, meaningful and humane collective spaces for learning, so enriching the lives of the children it serves.

elevations

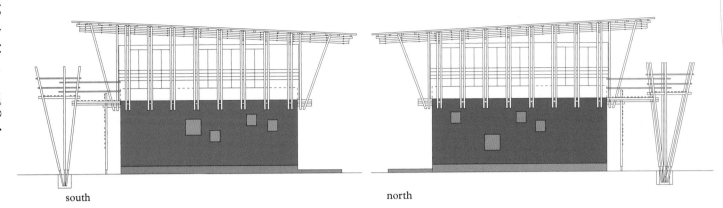

south   north

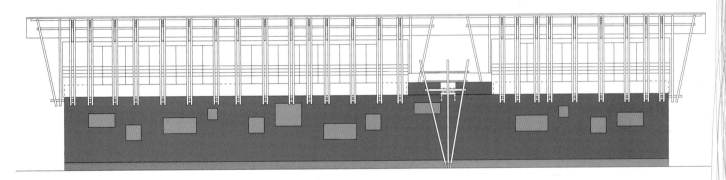

west

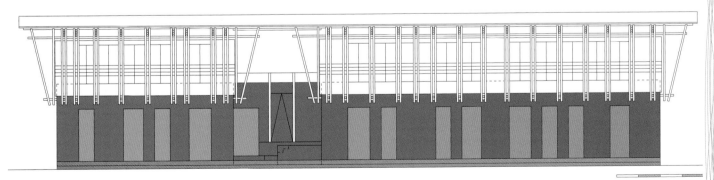

east   1.0 m

Project Description

The school is the fortunate result of a chain of events that began in 1997 when the designer, Anna Heringer, went to Bangladesh as a volunteer with a German NGO, Shanti. Although she returned to Europe after a year to begin her studies in architecture, she maintained her links with Dipshikha (Shanti's partner NGO in Bangladesh) and continued to be a regular visitor to their compound in Rudrapur, a village in the northwest of Bangladesh. It was on one of these visits that her input on expanding the existing educational facilities was sought.

The existing buildings had brick walls and thin pitched roofs. Dipshikha imagined that the new structure, as a representative building, would take a similar form. They initially resisted Anna's proposal for a mud-walled building, explaining that parents judge a school by its outward appearance – and a mud school would symbolise to most of them that they could not afford any better. Traditional mud construction is much maligned in the area. The typical farmer's mud house tends to last for only 10 to 15 years, is susceptible to fungus, and dark and dank inside.

Eventually, Dipshikha yielded to the irrefutable argument that the guiding principle of their development work – which is to recognise and develop locally available potential – should also be applied to the making of their school. The construction process would engage the local craftsmen, who would 'learn by doing', picking up new techniques that they could then use to improve the general standard and conditions of rural housing. The pupils and teachers would also be involved, so that they would understand the building and identify with it.

Working together with the Executive Director of Dipshikha, Paul Cherwa Tigga, Anna developed a programme for a mud-walled building incorporating technical improvements that would overcome the problems of the traditional structures. The development of the design formed the basis of Anna's diploma project at the University of the Arts in Linz in 2004. The next step was fundraising, which was coordinated by the German NGO, Shanti. Anna played an active role in this, as did many others in her home town, and a total of US$ 350,000 was raised for the school.

Teaching at the school is based on the METI (Modern Education and Training Institute) programme, which was initiated in Rudrapur in 1999 and is now being replicated in nearby Dinajpur and Osmanpur. There are two dimensions to the programme. The first is general education in line with the national curriculum, which covers subjects such as mathematics, languages, sciences, social studies and biology. These lessons take place in the morning, from 8.30 am to 1 pm. The afternoon, from 2.30 pm to 4.30 pm, is the time for teaching life skills, such as painting, songs, dance, writing sessions, clay modelling, handicrafts, role playing, games and sports.

These dual aspects are mirrored in the building, where two materials are used to create two very different atmospheres. The first floor is an open space – an overlook, a vantage point – shaped by bamboo, while the ground floor has earthen 'cave areas' where the children can retreat to read, reflect or meditate. The thick walls ensure a comfortable climate in the ground floor of the building. Sunlight and ventilation can be regulated through the use of shutters. A vertical garden facade shades the openings and protects the walls from erosion through rainfall; it also improves evaporation, which helps reduce the indoor temperature.

Traditional mud walls are formed with very wet loam. Here, an adapted technique called 'Wellerbau' was used. The wet loam is mixed with straw and applied to the wall in layers, each around 50–70 centimetres high. After drying for a couple of days the sides of the walls are trimmed with a sharp spade to obtain a regular flat surface. After a second drying period, a further layer can be added on top. The earth in this region is well suited to such construction and the stability of the mixture was improved by adding rice, straw and jute (cows and water buffalos did the work of treading in the mixture). A further vital technical improvement on traditional house construction was the introduction of a damp-proof course and a brick foundation.

The ceiling as well as the first floor is constructed mainly from bamboo, which is widely used by the locals for scaffolding, bridges and other structural components. In many instances, bamboo is better than other comparable materials such as wood or steel. It is light in weight and exhibits a high elasticity and tensile resistance, which makes it appropriate for seismic zones. Bamboo is fast-growing, comparatively low in cost, contributes to the aeration of other building elements, and is easy to handle and maintain. From an ecological point of view, it is also totally recyclable.

Three layers of bamboo sticks, bamboo boards and an earth filling make up the surface of the floor. The upper walls and roof are a frame construction using four layers of joined bamboo sticks and vertical and diagonal bamboo poles. Steel pins are fixed with nylon lashing (a variation on the traditional jute ropes) from the junction of the sticks. The walls are covered with slats of bamboo that allow diffused light as well as natural ventilation.

Since it is the local custom to sit on the floor, there is little need for interior furnishing apart from straw mats. Colourful drapes hung at ceiling level and in doorways soften the hard surfaces and give the light an interesting cast. Brightly painted doorways on the ground floor double as blackboards for the children to write and draw on.

The school, as a representative public building, has drawn many visitors and created a positive image for earth construction. The next phase of the development will involve the construction of prototype mud-walled houses as a model for rural living. As the designers say, 'We believe that architecture is more than shelter. It is ultimately connected with the creation of identity and self-confidence.'

Text adapted from a report
by Jimmy C.S. Lim

section

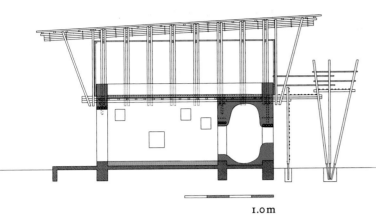

1.0 m

floor plans

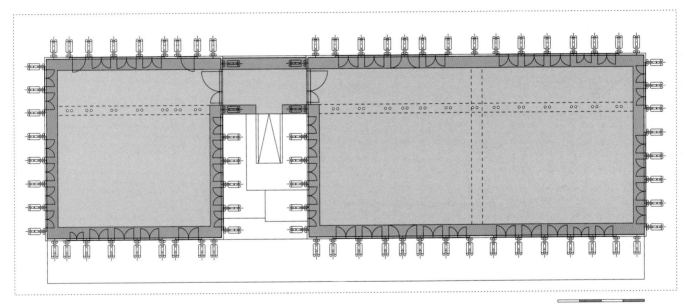

first floor

1.0 m

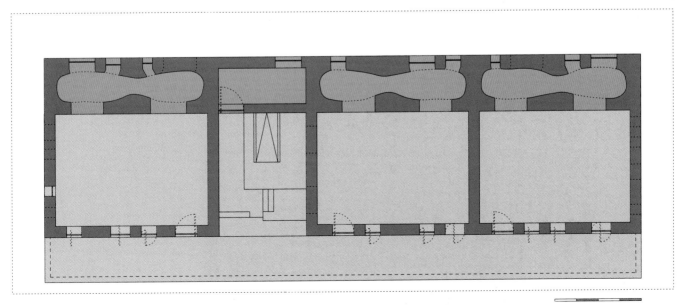

ground floor

1.0 m

School in Rudrapur
Dinajpur, Bangladesh

Client
Dipshikha/META non-formal
Education, Training and Research
Society for Village Development,
Bangladesh: Paul Cherwa Tigga,
executive director, Prodip Francis
Tigga, headmaster

Architects
Anna Heringer, Austria;
Eike Roswag, Germany

Supervisors
Sepal Debsharma, Afser Ali, Abu
Solaiman, Dipshikha, Bangladesh;
Emmanuel Heringer, carpenter,
basket weaver, bamboo consultant,
Germany, Stefanie Haider,
blacksmith, Germany

Civil Engineers
Ziegert Roswag Seiler (ZRS),
Germany: Christof Ziegert,
Uwe Seiler

Craftsmen
Mud work section: Reboti Roy,
Nikhil Chandra Roy, Buden
Chandra Roy, Aminul Islam, Apon
Chandra Roy, Suresh Chandra Roy,
Jitendra Nath Roy, Sonjib Roy.
Bamboo section: Romesh Roy, Fatik
Roy, Bimol Roy, Upendra Nath Roy,
Khokendra Nath Roy, Susen Roy,
Vhomol Chandra Roy, Bimol
Chandra Roy. Sontosh Purification,
carpenter (all in Bangladesh)

Project Data
Built area: 325 m²
Cost: US$ 22,835
Commission: January 2004
Design: March 2004–August 2005
Construction: September 2005–
December 2005
Occupancy: December 2005

Bibliography
*da! Architecture from and in Berlin
2006*, exhibition catalogue, German
Chamber of Architects in Berlin
Architectural Review, December 2006
architektur. aktuell, October 2006
bauwelt 32, 2006
Detail, April 2007
Flair, September 2006

Website
www.meti-school.de

Anna Heringer (b. 1977) studied
architecture at Linz University of the
Arts, Austria. Since 2004 she has
held a lectureship there, and is
project manager at BASE – habitat/
architektur konzepte, Linz University of the Arts. In 2006 she began
her doctoral studies at Munich
Technical University on strategies for
sustainable building in northern
Bangladesh. She is vice-chairwoman
of Shanti, a German-Bangladeshi
partnership founded in 1983 with
the aim of arranging exchange
programmes, for example the transfer of professional volunteers.

Eike Roswag (b. 1969), completed
his architectural studies at Berlin
Technical University in 2000, after
which he took on freelance architectural work and consultancies.
In 2003 he joined ZRS Architects and
Engineers to plan and build a variety
of projects using earth as a building
material. In 2006 he joined the staff
of Berlin Technical University and
founded Roswag & Jankowski
Architects Partnership.

Founded in 1978, Dipshikha –
Informal Education, Training and
Research Society for Village
Development is a Bangladeshi
development organisation set up to
encourage the independence of
communities in rural Bangladesh
through sustainable development.

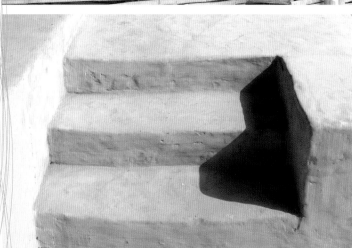

Ideas for Change

Sensitivity to Context

Negotiations

Changing the
Status Quo

Interventions

Architectural
Ethnography

Affective
Contribution

New Models
of Urbanism

Accretive
Urbanisation

Collaboration

Education

Excellence

Sustainability

Coherences

Transformations

Broader Context

Process

Humane Urban
Density

Dialogic *umma*

Contemporaneity

Translation and
Transition

Ecological Urbanism

The Aga Khan Awards for Architecture are generally intended for projects that are transformative in nature, that make an important social contribution to their respective communities and in the process make a significant contribution to architecture as well.

Apart from some examples of historic preservation, however, many of the selected buildings are built outside the context of a vital urban condition. In the absence of such context, the autonomy and the typological uniqueness of the buildings frame the primary parameters for their evaluation.

Buildings in dense urban settings therefore feature more rarely in the awards, as do public spaces that provide citizens with new spaces for interaction and socialisation. In the formation of contemporary urban developments in the Islamic world, it seems that less attention is given to the space between buildings, the very glue that binds the elements of a genuine public space. Why is that? Why is it so hard today to conceive of a compact, dense urbanism that would in some way parallel the best historic examples of the Islamic city?

It is true, of course, that the concept of the 'Islamic city' itself has been questioned by some scholars, who have drawn our attention to the local, site-specific origins of the older cities. Such cities are not based on a singular identifiable model, but have hybrid characteristics created by the way they cultivate the existing urban fabric through a process of addition and modification. This practice offers some challenges as well as some possible solutions to the contemporary situation.

In many respects, the conditions for testing new conceptions of urbanism seem unpromising. Some degree of experimentation does exist – a response to the unbridled opportunities offered to many international architects – but the results are variable. On the whole, development has been focused on branding a garish emulation of western modernity. There has been no systematic attempt to take up the challenge of constructing an alternative form of urbanism – one that could be inspired by the best of precedents, whether from the western or the Islamic worlds, one that would be innovative but, where necessary, specific to the region.

As testimony to what can be achieved in a very short time, architecturally and urbanistically, we have Dubai, an artifice capable of providing a futuristic oasis based on pure consumption, a cornucopia of gaudy luxury that already uses almost three times as much energy per person as the US – itself one of the worst culprits in terms of per-capita energy consumption. What is at stake here is not simply a shift from the tectonic to a thermodynamic paradigm in architecture, but a new form of practice that explores the reciprocities between built form and energy consumption at both the urban and the regional level.

More importantly, to anticipate, plan and take part in such a practice requires a new mind-set – what Guattari called a process of re-singularisation of existence. By this he meant that we, as individuals, must be ready for dissent. A social and political ecology, he argued, depends on the collective production of unpredictable and untamed 'dissident subjectivities' rather than the mass movement of like-minded people.

The future architecture of the Islamic world needs to take place within such a context of sustainable and ecological development. Urban ecology cannot be reduced to the single issue of cutting energy use (however important that may be). Rather, an ecological urbanism needs to incorporate an ethics of size, of social mix, of density and of public space. There is ample evidence to demonstrate that the wealthier portions of the population are continually expanding the size of the areas they inhabit. These supposed 'improvements' in lifestyle have a significant impact on the consumption of resources; they also aggravate the long-standing inequalities between the rich and the poor. Dubai, with its emphasis on signature architecture, has so far been rather good at concealing these disparities, but one has only to visit a city like Mumbai, where the worst shantytowns lie in the shadow of the most expensive developments, to see the stark contrasts that emerge with uncontrolled development. Perhaps the mere visibility of such a contrast is a more honest picture of reality. After all, who knows where they house all the workers who service an economy like Dubai's? It may be better to face the uncomfortable realities of the city than to present it as a simulacrum – a gigantic desiring machine not so different from Disneyland.

At the larger scale, it is the infrastructure of our cities that provides the best opportunities for constructing the framework for an urban environment that is spatially equitable and open to the participation of all citizens. If urban development is left primarily to the private sector, it is hard to envisage an appropriate funding of this infrastructure. Collaboration between public and private initiatives is thus one of the key mechanisms for the articulation of a public sphere of institutions and spaces that are networked to benefit the populace.

The design of such an environment – of an ecologically grounded urbanism – is itself a new form of research endeavour that relies in part on our understanding of earlier precedents, combined with new forms of collaboration between clients, users, architects, urbanists, landscape urbanists and other consultants. This situation is not unique to the Islamic world, yet the fact that many Islamic societies are only now undergoing significant and rapid development provides an important momentum for articulating an urbanism that can match the best traditions of architecture and engineering of the Islamic city.

Mohsen Mostafavi

Hybrid Identities

Cities that once hosted nations now host a rich array of 'cosmopolitans', brought together by the processes of globalisation. Cities are no longer singular 'wholes', but molecular compositions continually redefined by the people who occupy them. They no longer have a singular ideal identity provided by the nation, but are made up of diverse and active constellations that unite to co-habit the city in 'connected isolations'.

Within this post-national condition, cultures and societies are internally differentiated. In his discussion of the case for cultural contamination and cosmopolitanism, the philosopher Kwame Anthony Appiah argues that even in our world of opposing ideas, there are many similarities and shared values amongst individuals that transcend boundaries.[1] Through their cosmopolitan societies Cairo, Leeds, Istanbul and Kuala Lumpur are being drawn ever closer together. Hybrid identities and cultures are emerging through the 'intersection and combination' of identities with other identities (Ulrich Beck), which then determines social integration. Cosmopolitanism is generated through hybridity and the transformation that arises from new and unexpected combinations of cultures and ideas. Unlike universalist ideas that enforce one vision of reality, cosmopolitanism is avowedly pluralist.

Whereas the architecture of the city could once represent the singular nation, today it needs to embody multiplicity: in Appiah's words, 'human variety matters, cosmopolitans think, because people are entitled to options'. As architects we produce options in the form of buildings and, in doing so, we make decisions on behalf of future inhabitants. There is a limit to how many options an architect can programme into a building before it acquires a sense of the fallible, the imperfect or the provisional. Buildings are required to fit within a certain set of fixed requirements, their durability must even be guaranteed. Alternative options are ultimately introduced by people, the inhabitants.

There are many instances of people hybridising buildings and spaces through a reappropriation of use. The pedestrians who populate De Certeau's *The Practice Of Everyday Life* find subversive uses for architecture while walking in the city. The Sunday picnics of Filipino women under the raised lobby of Norman Foster's HSBC bank building in Hong Kong are another example of the reappropriation of architecture. Emerging extreme sports such as parkour, buildering or base jumping also reconfigure the urban environment as a field of play. However, this remains an opportunistic annexing of architecture for activities that the architect or urban designer has usually not foreseen or made any specific provision for.

Since buildings in their completed state are not conducive to Appiah's 'endless process of imitation and revision', the pursuit of cosmopolitanism should be diverted to the architectural process, to see if architecture can emerge out of the hybridisation of multiple forces and materials and, like people, be both unique (and local) and plural (and global). Earlier years of globalisation were captured by the architects of 'Deconstruction', who used collage to express diversity but failed to make new combinations or generate new ideas and identities in this way. Now that difference is found everywhere, it seems that the critical question for architecture has changed. Instead of declaring that differences are un-combinable, the point is to identify differences that are singular, look for connections, define systems of negotiation and find larger areas of consistency among these differentiated entities that can produce new hybrid organisations. Addressed to architecture, these issues question the way we relate parts to whole.

Architectural problems certainly do bring into play a multiplicity of forces. Many different types of material are involved in the design process, from wood and steel to programme, lifestyle, time, imagery, economy, context, atmosphere and culture. Any architectural process searches for a transversal connection across these diverse materials to form a design concept. This transversal link can integrate a range of specific materials, producing unique hybrid materialities. Alternatively, style can be pursued as a form of purity that overrides material specificities. The first leads to a process that constructs new identities through a hybridisation of material, the second produces 'style' as a pure concept deployed onto reality. Certainly, in the 1980s, architects pursued an approach in which the architectural product was based primarily on individual authorship or style. Having

16

witnessed the early stages of globalisation in the 1970s, they devised branding strategies to be applied wherever they might operate, thus maintaining a degree of consistency in the work of their practice. A critique that style produces 'global homogeneity' led architects in the 1990s to move away from imposing their idiosyncrasies onto the site and, instead, to develop projects from the local situation.

However, neither the proposal to derive each project purely from the situation every time nor stylistic approaches that insist on the same everywhere in themselves allow for the 'endless process of imitation and revision' that Appiah advocates. The architectural potential of Appiah's argument lies in the hybridisation of different existing domains to create new identities and therefore new knowledge over time. His proposal interestingly requires the coming together of the two earlier reactions to globalisation, so that the ongoing research of a practice intersects with the specificities of given projects to grow new identities that are unique to a situation, yet benefit and evolve from expertise and knowledge gained in other domains.

In all this, it is vital to avoid the sheer mixing that leads to stylistic eclecticism. Appiah's model applied to architecture needs to go beyond Venturi + Scott Brown's use of multiple sources from high and low culture, which tend towards the mixing of the original iconography rather than its integration. The Disney building by Michael Graves or the Chiat Day by Frank Gehry and Claus Oldenburg likewise fail to assimilate an original iconography into new productions, and simply lay one material on top of the other. In order to move beyond mere mixing and produce new hybrid materialities, we need to construct a mechanism whereby different architectural materials can hybridise, producing new material aggregates.

The main challenge for architects is to merge their own evolving expertise with the specificities of each project – the particularities of the site, economics, environmental issues, the agencies that inform the process or will later use the project. Given the opportunities for cross-cultural exchange, their expertise can travel across domains and hybridise with local cultures to breed new and unique identities. In line with Nicolas Bourriaud's proposals of Postproduction, in which new meanings and ideas are generated through the recycling, repositioning and reorientation of existing ideas,[2] architects can construct new hybrid materialities from the intersections of this diverse material. The architect's skills – rather than being applied to attach an artificial symbolism to each new project – can be exposed to materials that are not already internalised within his or her work, triggering new experimentation for the practice and producing new and unexpected combinations of material. In this way, the consumption of reality becomes a site of resistance, a tactic that allows ideas and products to be consumed to generate architectural opportunities that evolve knowledge as well as breed new identities.

Hybridisation suggests a completely different approach to how one constructs architectural identities or 'wholes'. As opposed to starting from an imagined whole (as is the case with stylistic approaches), in hybrid materials the whole is grown out of the hybridisation of the parts, akin to the way hybrid identities evolve in individuals. Hybridisation transforms fixed architectural categories and unleashes possibilities for architectural experimentation. Many recipients of the Aga Khan Award have been the result of such a process: the hybridisation of a high-rise with Malaysian culture (Petronas Towers), a school in Burkina Faso bringing together local builders and German education, a library in Cairo and skills of Norwegian architects (Bibliotheca Alexandrina), a high-rise housing structure with traditional monsoon windows (Moulmein Rise in Singapore), an airport terminal with Bedouin tents in membrane structure (Haj Terminal), a school with vaulted structure in stone (Fazlur Rahman Khan Engineering School)… In each case the hybridisation with external material introduces certain transformative forces into each typology which cause the type to mutate into new forms of organisation.

Farshid Moussavi

1. K. Anthony Appiah, *Cosmopolitanism, Ethics in a World of Strangers*, Princeton University Press 2004.
2. Dennis Kaspori, 'A Communism of Ideas', *Archis* no. 3, 2003.

The Memory of a City / The City as a Repository for Memories

Memory and Identity

Societies construe their histories from pasts reclaimed together. Through the telling and remembrance of these, a collective consciousness is formed. A virtual 'memory space' is created where diverse experiences and moral concepts are taken up, but also suppressed. The virtual discourse on memory and remembrance also needs real things as materialised reference points, to give meaning to the imaginary material. This is why objects that are handed down, and exist outside their time, are preserved. For the historical material to reach from the past into the present, however, it must be continually recontextualised, reinterpreted and renegotiated as being of intrinsic value to society. Only in this way can it provide inspiration for the future.

Materialised Memory

One of the most potent places for collecting and keeping the curious things of the past is, besides the museum, the city itself. In the space of the city, the alien is incessantly assimilated into the existing and the known. Cities are documents of the processes by which differences are redeemed and negated. They embody the traces of history in the form of streets, squares and buildings. Then again, these are subject to unrelenting change through new uses and redevelopment. In the city, the potentials, ambitions, interests, desires and passions existing in a society are reflected in a concentrated form. The way in which differences coexist side by side can be seen in buildings and the way they evolve over time – provided ideologies, acts of aggression or natural catastrophes do not result in their radical destruction. Buildings also disappear for other reasons – because they have lost their function, because they stand in the way of current needs, or because they hold a significance that contradicts the *Zeitgeist*. Every city is marked by the conflicts associated with these facets. In the urban tableau, the claims on the past, present and future are negotiated anew by each generation.

Making decisions about which memories and meanings are particularly worthy of protection has, through the course of history, led to the development of oft-modified moral concepts and criteria, a 'practice of remembrance'. With this in mind, one may see the city in the metaphorical sense as a book in which innumerable past, present and future authors illustrate their ideologies in the forms of architecture and space. To analyse the 'city as text' means, above all, to deconstruct the wide-ranging images, memories, ideas and perceptions of those things that are alien – those things associated with or attributed to a city – so that their symbolic dimensions may be understood. In this, historical culture and the culture of remembrance have a significant role to play.

Cities are, in effect, public stagings of history and remembrance: they reflect the prevailing philosophies and economic interests. A solid commitment is required on the part of the people and institutions who renovate and care for the historic built fabric, so that the past may be imagined in a literal sense, so that it may be interpreted and understood. If, however, the motivation that allows history to be used for the purpose of self-image is lacking, every built monument is in a precarious position and every process of salvage – however complex the restoration – only temporary. In addition, every historic building and every city has to struggle against an all-encompassing pursuit of 'newness', as all societies strive first to seem young, strong and contemporary.

For the role of the 'old' to be acknowledged, one also needs a general social understanding of the importance of history for the present and for the future. History probably holds this social importance all over our world. The question is, how strong in each different place and time is the social need to preserve the traces of history? Another issue arises when the opposite impulse prevails, and the primary goal is to eliminate any building culture as quickly as possible. Where there is no generalised need for a life that includes a materialised history as a matter of course, every monument protection measure is quickly seen as an alien and objectionable intervention, or even simply as irrelevant. In order for buildings or urban ensembles to be valued by an urban society to the extent that they are understood as a cultural legacy and conserved, a broad social, political, economic or cultural consensus must be developed. This can be a long, drawn-out process, taking years or even decades, but without it every monument is under threat.

Demolition or Conservation?

Historic preservation, as it emerged in Europe in the late nineteenth and early twentieth century, was a reaction against the rapid and comprehensive revolution brought by industrial modernisation, where the 'old' was seen as a threat to the new requirements of functionality and efficiency and at risk of comprehensive destruction. As a counterbalance to the upheavals of industrialisation, historic preservation brought the ideas of nation and continuity to the fore. An ideational increase in the value of one's own history and the material evidence of that history led to mechanisms for preservation being instituted and incorporated into municipal administration structures.

In the contemporary context of economic globalisation, it is the field of tourism that emphasises cultural autonomy as a locational advantage. At the same time, this globalisation has contributed to the universalisation of the European philosophy of historic preservation. The programme of UNESCO, for example, has a crucial influence on what is listed as a World Heritage Site. UNESCO's professed goal, and that of many other initiatives, is to preserve cultural variety under the conditions of globalisation and liberalisation. However, whether and how this goal is taken on and interpreted across the globe is also of vital importance.

European societies, particularly in the twentieth century, have developed a number of partial, heterogeneous and often contradictory reasons to legitimise something in terms of its historical value. As such, a building can be valuable because it is especially beautiful or ugly, because it is original or typical for its time, or because its history is associated with important people or events. It can also be valuable because it was once popular or extremely unpopular, because it was designed as a monument from the start, or even because it was first perceived as a monument because its construction was particularly expensive. The reasons for considering a building or an ensemble of buildings worthy of protection are manifold, and there is no general set of rules. What is important is that the monument represents something unusual rather than everyday. However, this in itself means that the monument's position is precarious and always open to question.

Whether or not a building can really have historical importance ultimately depends on whether a lasting international, national and local consensus can be reached on its distinctive character, confirming its status as a building worthy of preservation or restoration. Thus it is only after the renovation of a building – when the city and its residents assume responsibility for its care – that the true survival of the building becomes an issue. For then it becomes clear whether the attempts to register the building in the collective consciousness and create a supportive atmosphere have been successful, or whether, conversely, it is seen as a remote and alien 'implant' and ultimately rejected.

Any project that perceives the historical site as an expression of isolated charitable concerns is almost always doomed from the outset. It is therefore necessary – particularly in regions and federal states where the concept of upgrading material things is new – to introduce site-protection measures on a cautious and broad basis. It is essential to communicate the reasons why a particular building or part of town is important enough to one's own history and to human experience to be preserved. At the same time, the right conditions must be created locally whereby projects, even if they are based on the wishes of others, are appreciated for their qualitative contribution to the revalorising of the city.

This calls not only for a long-term economic concept for the post-renovation period but also for a process that enables all those involved to reflect upon and if necessary modify their own position and the stated reasons for protection. Especially in the world's poorer countries, cities must also actively support these initiatives – a difficult undertaking, as they often lack the necessary organisational, staffing and financial resources. The bureaucratic aspect also requires simplification.

Every historic spatial organisation or work of architecture can be seen as a gift and a special testimony to a city's public space. As such, each city must be able or prepared to bear this distinctiveness – this legacy – and to accept it as a challenge and take responsibility for it.

Omar Akbar

Many Modernities

It does not necessarily take an academic to establish that our world is complex. There are two aspects to this complex world. One is the complexity arising in our daily lives and the representations that we make in them. The growing mobility of people across the planet is resulting in an ever more visible hybridity. Each of us carries layers of identities that we use to interact with the multitude of choices and tasks that represent the tangible elements through which the complexities of the world are translated. Meanwhile, the growing potential for cross-cultural encounters, the reality of talking and listening to each other, makes us more aware, not only of the existence of a plurality of references and beliefs, but also of their integration into – or exclusion from – power relations that are not necessarily visible, physical. This situation does not preclude the possibility that some actors will imagine that they can disturb existing power relations – and that they will in fact have the means to do so. This duality of powerlessness and having tremendous power, at both micro and macro levels, has become another ingredient of the complexity of the world that we share.

In our cross-cultural world, these layers of inclusion or exclusion, of acceptance or denial, are sometimes seen through the prism of modernity. In one view of the complexity of the world, the major issue is the desirability or inevitability of the path towards modernity, in the sense of establishing western values and modes of social organisation. Francis Fukuyama's 'End of History' thesis, notwithstanding his relative revision of some of his premisses, aspires to and justifies this logic of inevitability. It implies the victory of liberal democracy after the Cold War: the absence of competition between superpowers makes the world a better (albeit more 'boring') place.

A contrasting perspective is offered by the political scientist Samuel P. Huntington, who argues that conflicts will arise along cultural rather than ideological lines, leading to a clash of the world's major civilisations – western, Islamic, Latin American, African, Buddhist, Orthodox, Chinese, Hindu and Japanese.

Despite the differences between these approaches, both foresee everything being subsumed into a unifying western value system, either because of an acceptance of its legitimacy (Fukuyama), or as a consequence of confronting it (Huntington).

This leads us to ask: Who is absorbing whom? And into what? There are two elements to this question, and one might give two answers.

The first kind of answer emerged from the Covenant of the League of Nations (1919), in the form of the Mandates system, where the development of colonised countries was supervised by advanced nations upholding 'a sacred trust of civilisation'. Another process of inclusion works by imposing changes on other people's way of being, taking them away from who they are and bringing 'them' into 'our' world. An extension of this process is the imposition of 'modernity' on 'traditional' societies.

One understanding of the expansion of modernity describes a hegemonic process based on the unchecked advance – and full acceptance – of the western version of modernity. However, other interpretations of modernity are possible. Differences between cultures, between peoples, have given rise to different types of modernity – what we might call multiple modernities.

In this context it is important to note how non-European societies have challenged the hegemony of modernity, causing transformations to occur and new questions to emerge. This critical modernity, or counter modernity, enables them to be selective about which elements of modernity to adopt; it leaves room, in the process of development and modernisation, for a society's own distinct traditions.

The social impact of modernity has been more intense, and more far-reaching, than that of any other movement or ideology in human history. One of the consequences of this process has been the birth of modern international structures – multi-centred and heterogeneous systems generated by dynamic and continuously changing relations between cultures. These structures share many common characteristics, but also evince differences among themselves.

Thus hegemonic modernity has always existed alongside critical modernity (which lies within hegemonic modernity) and counter modernity (which lies outside it). The interaction between them creates tensions and contradictions.

We can note three aspects of the 'original' modernity that developed in the west. The first aspect is structural and organisational, relating to growing urbanisation, industrialisation and communication networks. The second is the institutional aspect, namely the development of the modern nation-state as a new polity, of national collectivities and capitalist political economies. The final aspect is modernity's distinct cultural programme, which is closely related to the specific structural modes of major arenas in social life.

Sociological analyses of modernisation and the convergence of modern societies tend to assume that hegemonic and homogenising tendencies will prevail in the west, and that modernity will continue to expand through time and space. Regardless of circumstances, all modern societies are supposed to take similar paths.

Yet modern societies are creating new interpretations of different dimensions of modernity, leading to the development of different cultural agendas. The original theory of modernity formulated in earlier decades has also come under criticism. Some have insisted that modernity has already come to an end (a theory criticised by scholars such as Jürgen Habermas). Even these radical reinterpretations constitute inherent components of the culture of modernity. Each activity against modernisation also connotes the nature of modernity.

In sum, cultures and civilisations are constantly changing through a process of dialogue. The notion of modernity (initially created in western societies) has been accepted and rearranged by non-western societies, taking on forms such as Islamic modernity, Confucian modernity, and so on.

Modernity has spread throughout most of the world, but not according to a single pattern. How it expands depends on the historical experience of the specific civilisation. One of the important things in today's scene is the continuous interaction among civilisations around modernity, including attempts at its radical rejection (the legitimacy of criticism is explicitly recognised). Today's multiple modernities share many common components and mutual reference points. They are continuously evolving, unfolding, giving rise to new problematics and reinterpretations of the basic premises of modernity.

If modernity can be plural, if the tangible and intangible elements of lived environments can have pluralistic logic and dynamics, can the makers of the built environment be open to such a multitude of modernities?

Modjtaba Sadria

Afterward

The Aga Khan Award for Architecture has had a powerful effect on the lives of many people. Attention has correctly focused on the benefits for those who use or live in the buildings that have won an award. As an architect, though, I was interested in the award's effect on the architects' lives and careers, and in particular its effect on the younger architects. So I wrote to Han Tümertekin and Francis Kéré, who were winners during the 2004 cycle when I was a juror. Both of these architects won awards for relatively small but deeply thoughtful and beautifully executed buildings that could be recognised as significant contributions to the quality of architecture in the Muslim world.

Han Tümertekin's B2 house is a hillside house for two brothers that builds on and reimagines the vernacular stone houses of northern Turkey. It sits easily in its village surroundings but simultaneously proclaims a new vision.

Francis Kéré brought to his village in Burkina Faso the knowledge that he had gained studying in Germany. His work embraces traditional building techniques – formed mud bricks and simple steel welding – to create a new primary school that is at once elegant, environmentally correct and deeply humane.

I asked three questions:
What was the best thing and the worst thing about winning this award?
Has winning the award affected your practice and if so, how?
What are you working on now that really interests you?

I wrote with some concern, because huge attention relatively early in one's career can often become a burden.

This answer came from Han.

The best thing about winning the award was entering an international network of people who are passionate about their work.

The award has not affected my personal approach to architecture, but it has transformed others' interest in my work into trust. I had already started being involved in more commissions, in large-scale and international projects. Winning the award accelerated this process. It led to the extensive publication of my work, which heightened interest in what I was doing.

The Aga Khan Award's networking structure enabled me to lecture, to be a visiting critic and jury member in distinguished academic institutions and circles of architecture.

Right now we are doing some interesting large-scale urban projects and individual houses. One project is about renovating a part of the city centre, and there are two shopping malls, one in the heart of the city, the other on the periphery. We are involved in a housing development in Bodrum where we're collaborating with international architects and I'm also building an individual house in an olive grove on the Aegean coast, as well as some houses in Geneva.

This answer came from Francis.

There is no question that winning the Aga Khan Award has changed my life in ways I never imagined possible. After the press review I was confronted with a flood of emails asking for information about the school building.

Students from all over the world – from the USA and Canada to Europe and South Africa – were looking at the building as an example of contemporary African architecture, of sustainable architecture and design. And all of them were looking to me in order to get more information.

Because of the award I moved swiftly from being an unknown person to being a sought-after professional. It is an unbelievable story.

But this story will only have a happy ending when I can tap all the positive impact of winning the award and make more projects for the benefit of the people of my home village.

It is clear that the award has had a great effect on the lives and careers of both of these architects. It has brought them into a larger world and given them a voice that will be listened to. Even if their future work does not directly touch the Muslim world, they will forever be connected to this award, and their success will bring added lustre to it.

This connection of the award to the larger architectural world is crucial because it speaks of the marriage of 'high' design with ethics. Too often, good intentions are realised in the form of mediocre architecture. There's a general attitude that says that it doesn't have to be so good if it's for a good cause.

We must demand that good intentions are expressed by the highest level of design. In this way, the quality of the aspiration can be matched by the quality of the built work. This, for me, is the basis of the Aga Khan Award for Architecture. It is what I believe in, and it is why it has been an honour and a challenge to have been involved.

Billie Tsien

Thoughts about the Award Process

Architecture fuses together poetic ideas, inert materials, physical site and social conditions. Architecture trades on its ability to touch and shape people's lives in profound and meaningful ways. Around the world, no matter where it is being practised, architecture is a complex discipline.

In January and June of 2007, I was honoured to be one of nine jury members invited to spend several days in an elegant boardroom in Geneva, focusing on ways that built architecture impacts on the Muslim world. Our attention was directed at the 343 projects submitted for consideration to the 2007 Aga Khan Award for Architecture. Each jury member was required to do plenty of homework prior to arriving in Geneva. There were thick binders full of background information to go through. My eyes adjusted slowly, over a period of several months. The Muslim world covers many continents, numerous climatic zones and specific regions of the globe. I became intimately aware of the enormous challenges and the hopeful opportunities of building in towns and cities like Koudougou, Beirut, Addis Ababa, Rada, Bandar Seri Iskandar, Singapore, Shibam, Nicosia and Rudrapur. My experience on this jury has recalibrated my senses. Because of the Aga Khan Award, I have been inspired to remap my world.

Lateral Conversations

Most architecture award juries – and I have sat on countless design juries in North America and Europe – bring together architects who review photographic images of built work and then select projects which reflect their collective vision of architectural excellence. The 2007 Aga Khan Awards for Architecture brought together five architects from around the world, as well as a historian, an artist, a curator and a literary theorist. Our task was to discuss, to interpret and to better understand the changing landscape of the Muslim world. In the course of our numerous jury sessions, I became aware that architects were also painters, that curators were also poets, and that everyone in the room was a teacher. We all listened and learned from the distinct voices around the table. The jury's definition of architectural excellence was constantly being challenged, defined and redefined. The winning projects were not easily decided. They *emerged* from the breadth of our lateral conversations.

Deep Vertical Knowledge

No other architectural awards programme in the world sends independent reviewers to all parts of the globe to visit the jury's shortlisted projects. No other architectural awards programme in the world brings the same independent reviewers to the awards jury to share their first-hand observations and insights about the physical and social context of the built work. The reviewers' personal field experience enabled the jury to build a knowledge base for each and every project. This is fundamental to what I'll call the vertical gathering of knowledge afforded by the Aga Khan Award.

The jury was made aware of the physical data, design and construction process, cultural contribution, construction schedule and cost, technical developments and social relevance for every project under consideration. We discussed the design intent and the design process, as well as the design results. We understood the varying roles of the contractors, builders and craftsmen in each project. We recognised the many types of strong individuals and client groups involved in commissioning work, as well as the complex nature of the design teams that are needed to realise any built project. The depth of our understanding of all of the shortlisted projects allowed the premiated projects to *emerge* from our deep vertical knowledge base.

Building Community

How can architecture continue to play a vital role in building community throughout the Muslim world? We saw many projects that suffered because they adopted a foreign or 'borrowed' language of architecture and did not carefully consider the communities that they serve.

As a counterpoint to this kind of placelessness, we need to support and celebrate ways of building community that derive from a deep understanding of the local culture and building traditions but simultaneously address the layered complexities of our modern world. The discipline of architecture needs to nurture alternative models of practice that link committed designers directly with local people, allowing them to engage in projects that have the capacity to build and transform communities.

At the Central Market in Koudougou, the building of a full-sized prototype of one market bay out of local compressed earth (*banco*) demonstrates an alternative way of working with local community groups. As a vehicle for communicating ideas, it allowed Swiss architects and engineers working for an international development agency to build up a truly participatory design process involving the local people. The market they created together has become a crucial piece of the town's infrastructure, a noble building for meeting and exchange that has transformed the lives of the people who use it – including the 600 women who regularly rent its market stalls and the 140 licensed masons trained during its construction. In this case, architecture succeeds and even triumphs as a collective act.

A new two-storey school in rural Bangladesh comes out of a young woman's understanding of the local community after she spent a year in the village as a volunteer. She combines her formal design training in architecture with her commitment to the community. A knowledge transfer takes place between a committed designer and a specific community which enables an exemplary building to emerge. The final result of their collective efforts is a joyous and sustainable building that serves its community well.

At no time in human history has the potential for architecture to shape our world been greater than it is today. The winners of the 2007 Aga Khan Award are all exemplary projects in their complexity. Each and every one of them has shown us that when given a chance, the human spirit is capable of transforming the world around us. There is much to be learned from their built forms. Perhaps the most valuable lesson, however, has to do with the way that architects can truly engage with the Muslim world even before they start to design.

Brigitte Shim

Architecture Retimed

In the context of a globalised practice of architecture, it is often asked how a project designed abroad may relate to the place in which it is built. Parallel to this relevance to place, another question concerns how architecture may be of its time, how it gains contemporaneity. During the jury discussions for the Aga Khan Award, we thought about the ways in which projects in the Islamic world are culturally specific, and of our time, in order to establish parameters for their evaluation.

As we look for new means of operating within modernity and locality, we may refute polarised categories – both the unquestioning modernist faith in technological progress and the rebound into a representational contextualism. We may consider, too, how the idea of place could be extended to the notion of an inverse locality, for projects built for heterogeneous Muslim communities living alongside other cultures in western cities. Having witnessed too many unsuccessful renditions of vernacular quick-fixes – collage domes and arches on cultural centres and mosques – we need to ask: In what ways can architectural projects respond positively and clearly to the more fluid post-colonial geographies that Islamic localities are now a part of, either as host places or as integrated guest sites? What is the nature of their affiliations to time and place?

In some respects, the linkage of displacement with locality has proved a productive means of over-coming the essentialising polarities of modern vs vernacular, western vs non-western, contemporary vs historic architecture. On another level, there is still a need to identify innovative translations of these displacements. New matrices of technological progress, economy, relevance, familiarity and desirability need to be found, which go beyond the oppositions of formal and typological plan, two-dimensional facade and three-dimensional abstract form, local techniques and modern technologies. To achieve this, architecture and its related disciplines have to explore the processes that generate new discursive formations and practices.

Crossed Disciplines

One set of discursive practices explores spaces, technologies and construction processes that cross disciplinary boundaries. Individual projects of architecture now intersect more critically with urbanism, landscape architecture, structural engineering and environmental design. Here, locality lies within the discipline, and displacement is triggered by the shifts between geometries, technologies and constructive logics.

Two examples of such projects in the 10th award cycle are the rehabilitation of Nicosia and the Samir Kassir Square in Beirut. In Nicosia, the adoption of a single masterplan by three generations of politicians on both sides of the divided city has created shared strategies for the conservation of cultural monuments, for an integrated infrastructure, and for the design of a new cohesive streetscape. This is an important, hopeful project of architecture and urbanism, acting as a cultural force and a catalyst for political change.

In Beirut, Samir Kassir Square combines radically contemporary design thinking with the preservation of two important old trees. It uses an embedded water tank and a deck to construct an environmental artefact and a three-dimensional public space. Its architecture stands apart from identifying typologies, activating contingent forces of topography and infrastructure to construct a new public space. Despite its small scale, the project creates a magnetic space that embodies a contradiction of contested localities. It is at once a public space for the community – a place for political engagement – and a space of inner calm for the individual.

Retimed Material Technologies

Another set of practices incorporate contemporary technologies into their structure and materials while finding innovative intersections with local techniques. In contrast to modern technology's fast-paced changes, vernacular practices have slower, more accumulated formations, as well as varying degrees of tolerances. By translating traditional structural and material logics into contemporary means of construction, these projects find new iterations of the original designs that define retimed parameters for contemporaneity and local desirability. The use of new materials, the reworking of traditional materials into new forms, and the combination of local materials with new structures or new geometries all produce a range of iterative transformations. Moving beyond the simple accommodation of local processes to frame new parameters for design, these projects participate in forces of renovation; they retime and reterritorialise both modern and vernacular materials and technologies.

The Dutch Embassy in Addis Ababa is a strong example of such engagement between contemporary architecture and the found landscape of another culture's time and place. Its form has a raw character – at once modern and archaic – shaped by local earth and local labour and by the use of handmade formwork for the concrete. The school in Rudrapur is an extraordinary instance of a project that makes simple yet inventive use of locally available resources. Working only with rammed straw-reinforced mud and bamboo, the project creates an elegant building which applies professional precision to local techniques and physical labour. The school transforms the lineaments and geometries of local space, finds new approximations for local materials, and generates alternative economies for the production of a retimed modern plan.

Environmental Gauge

The environmental gauge offers another set of questions for the siting of projects. How do local typologies, practices and resources measure against the development of modern materials and methods of environmental control? Given more complex programmes and urban densities, it seems that neither traditional nor modern techniques in themselves produce a wholly satisfactory response. Tradition may ensure economy and locally appropriate design, but the new technologies of mechanical services produce the desired continuous control. In innovative environmental design, the crossing of the two drives the formation of spaces and material detailing.

At the University of Technology Petronas the grouping of buildings under a continuous canopy produces shaded open-air pedestrian routes around the campus. The careful choice of materials for the external skin(s) and intricate detailing allow otherwise standard building types to achieve flexibility in relation to changes in use. A close collaboration between the international and the Malaysian architects ensured that the processes of fabrication and construction were integrated into local practices.

In the residential tower at Moulmein Rise in Singapore, traditional monsoon windows and perforated screens are realised in new configurations and materials. The effect is both aesthetic, in the form of finely detailed private balconies, and practical, in that it improves natural ventilation and so reduces the need for air-conditioning. The narrow depth of the plan and the imaginative reappraisal of planning guidelines enable this commercial development to achieve a new design language and economy.

Finally, each of the projects selected in this cycle was recognised to have readjusted absolute notions of contemporaneity and locality. Rather than belonging to our time through their use of new technologies or materials, or their affiliation to sites of dispersed and displaced localities, their design methods and processes create a singular time and singular locations through a retimed contemporaneity. In each, one detects a hopeful confidence along with the delicate vulnerabilities and risks found in any new locality. In framing these paradoxes, the projects reflect our recognition of the promise of architecture as a universal cultural force in a continual practice of retiming modernity.

Homa Farjadi

Highlighting a Cross-Section

For the past month I have been subconsciously resisting the idea of summarising my thoughts on the winning projects of the 10th cycle of the Aga Khan Award for Architecture. Perhaps such resistance results from the difficulty of condensing the complexity within the nature of each project or the vast parameters by which we conducted our quest. After examining so many projects it is very difficult (if not impossible) to describe the status of architecture in the Muslim world in a manner that would comply with the view of this world as the opaque and monolithic Other. Yet simultaneously it is also very difficult to clearly define the progression or merits of the built environment of this world.

In the face of such a reality the process and measures of evaluation become a multiply determined matrix, where each project dictates its own particular parameters of analysis, distancing itself from possible comparisons with other works that may share similar functions or at times fall into the same category. Evaluation in this sense also requires a willingness on the part of both jury members and technical reviewers to redefine their subjectivity and personal formation accordingly.

The process of examining the nominated projects revealed an immense diversity of cultural environments across the Muslim world, between their geographies, conditions of practice and identities, between ideas that form positions within a locality and within the world. The differences were both radical and subtle, confronting us with the task of tailoring the instruments by which we read architecture in order to go beyond form and aesthetics – and most importantly beyond a 'global' discourse of what Architecture (with a capital 'A') is or should be. The danger in this, however, is the loophole – perhaps an inherent one – that allows forces outside the design dimension of architecture to place more emphasis on the conditions of a project than on the project itself and how it actually operates within those conditions. In fact, this was a topic that often recurred in our discussions in various forms, demanding further scrutiny and understanding.

I believe an attempt was made to seek works that have a certain transformative power, facilitating responsible change – to find projects that could be seen as paradigms, demonstrating architecture's capacity to assimilate problems and challenges and, by internalising them, convert them into strategies that transform by virtue of negotiation and not by imposition. Excellence in this mixture of elements, sought by jurors of diverse backgrounds, became a malleable and relative entity, which at times could withstand all types of measures and at others not. In this context, standards of excellence were not constant factors but rather a set of variables or contingencies.

The selection process bears a great resemblance to the operating methods of some of the projects – working with what is at hand, filtering and bringing to light hidden potentials, seeking that which is conducive to the enhancement of the human condition. As a corollary to this, one is forced to realise that the current reality of architecture in the Muslim world – in spite of its vastness – is still very problematic. It seems that potentially seminal works of architecture in Muslim societies remain inert and sterile in the margins, hardly ever having an impact on architectural production or the norms of practice in general. Experimentation is a rarity, often confused with style or expression, and often limited to private initiatives that never seep into public policies. Last, but not least, there is a dearth of urban interventions that deal with the city or human settlement on a viable level.

The hope is to counteract this reality by emphasising the importance of these projects as samples extracted from a vast cross-section of a fertile terrain. These pointers and markers are essential for further developments and evolutions. They will, I hope, provoke change on a much larger scale – the scale of mental disposition.

Sahel Al-Hiyari

Sustainability

The Aga Khan Award for Architecture is unique. No other architectural award in the world comes anywhere near its depth and breadth. Its strength, and that which distinguishes it from other awards, is that it is given to a work of built architecture, often defined in the widest sense of the word, rather than to a particular individual or group.

At the outset, a pool of around one thousand nominators propose hundreds of projects from around the world. From these the jury selects a shortlist of projects, which are thoroughly researched and photographed and then reviewed in depth by a third party, who in turn presents these projects back to the jury. This is what further differentiates the Aga Khan Award – the jury does not just review the submitted material. Following the presentations by the reviewers, the jury further deliberates about the criteria for judging and the message that will be implicitly conveyed to the world's community of architects by the winning projects. In any award cycle, the set of premiated projects and the role of the jury are crucial. The jury's message is seen as indicative of the pressing architectural and environmental issues of the day, defining the *Zeitgeist* of the architectural world to practitioners and others in the Muslim world and elsewhere.

If there is a weakness in this awards process, it is that the list of projects for review has already been assembled by the award office by the time the jury convenes. When the jury first meets, it is like a chef who has not gone to the market to see the catch of the day; it has to work with whatever is available in the larder. The jury becomes responsible for viewing vital contemporary issues through the lens of projects that may have been designed up to a decade ago, since only completed projects are eligible. Thus the critical architectural and environmental issues of the day may well be obscured or not evident, at least until the next awards cycle.

In assessing this current cycle, it became clear that there were insufficient projects that address sustainability. Al Gore's now well-known film of his Powerpoint presentation about climate change, 'An Inconvenient Truth', has increased global concern about the direct impact of the human built environment on the climate, and made evident the critical nature of the ecological agenda. Evidence of worldwide environmental devastation and climate change is ubiquitous, with the conspicuously diminishing polar ice caps, the loss of snowfall on Mount Kilimanjaro, the rise in sea levels and a whole host of other issues. Many designers and political leaders now recognise that they must confront the issue of saving the natural environment; the master jury, too, recognises that the Aga Khan Award must address this issue with urgency. The question presented to us in our role as jurors was: How do we design for a sustainable future in the Muslim world?

We first run the risk of 'greenwash' – the belief that if an architect and his MEP engineers stuff a building with enough eco-technology systems and gadgets (such as photovoltaic modules or solar collectors, rainwater harvesting and recycling systems, etc.) they will have an instant green building. Of course nothing is further from the truth. Green design is much more than that. It is an attempt to integrate our human built environment seamlessly and benignly with the natural environment, which calls for an understanding of the processes that take place in local ecosystems and in the biosphere before the insertion of any new built system.

However, sustainability is not only the concern of architects and designers. Companies and businesses (who ultimately commission architects and designers to make built works) must seek to understand the environmental consequences of industry, engage with environmentally benign processes and seek new ecologically responsive solutions, strategies, business models and production systems. If we create a built environment that is truly ecologically responsive, it will alter the way we work and our current ecologically profligate lifestyle, and of course the way we plan, design, build, use and eventually recycle our built environment, which includes not just our buildings but also infrastructures and everything that we make (such as refrigerators, clothes, toys, etc.), as well as those human activities that impinge on the natural environment. The nominators and jury of the next Aga Khan Award should vitally address this.

Kenneth Yeang

Beauty is Truth

'Beauty is truth, truth beauty' – that is all
Ye know on earth, and all ye need to know.

John Keats, 'Ode on a Grecian Urn'

One could say that we need to look for beauty in a building as the first expression of creativity – beauty of space, pattern, light and shadow, beauty of texture and surface.

To judge architecture from the perspective of a visual artist, I needed to ask myself some questions: What is architecture? Is it made by us, the people who use it? Does it shape us and create who we are? This enquiry led me to look at architecture in a particular way. I realise that our towns and cities are the windows to our unconscious, our homes the frames for our lives. As we look through them, these windows and frames colour our understanding of the world.

In discussing architectural projects across the Muslim world for the award, I recognised that Muslim societies have diverse cultures and different realities. What connects them, most often, are economics and politics – and the growing gap between rich and poor, with access to education for the rich, and few opportunities for the poor.

Architecture clearly has the power to influence and change people's lives. Buildings that offer spaces for contemplation and reflection, wonder and beauty, can create a culture of understanding and acceptance. By participating in the imaginative shaping and development of the built environment, we can all play our part in creating inclusive societies that challenge prejudices and make a shared space for all people of all faiths.

The great Islamic cultures of the past were famous for their inclusiveness and tolerance. This is perhaps best illustrated in the following lines by Ibn Arabi, a great Muslim philosopher and poet who lived in Andalusia during the twelfth century:

My heart can take on any form:
A meadow for gazelles,
A cloister for monks,
For the idols, sacred ground
Ka'ba for the circling pilgrims,
The tablets of the Torah,
The scrolls of the Qu'ran
I profess the religion of love;
Wherever its caravan turns along the way,
That is the belief,
The faith I keep.

Shirazeh Houshiary

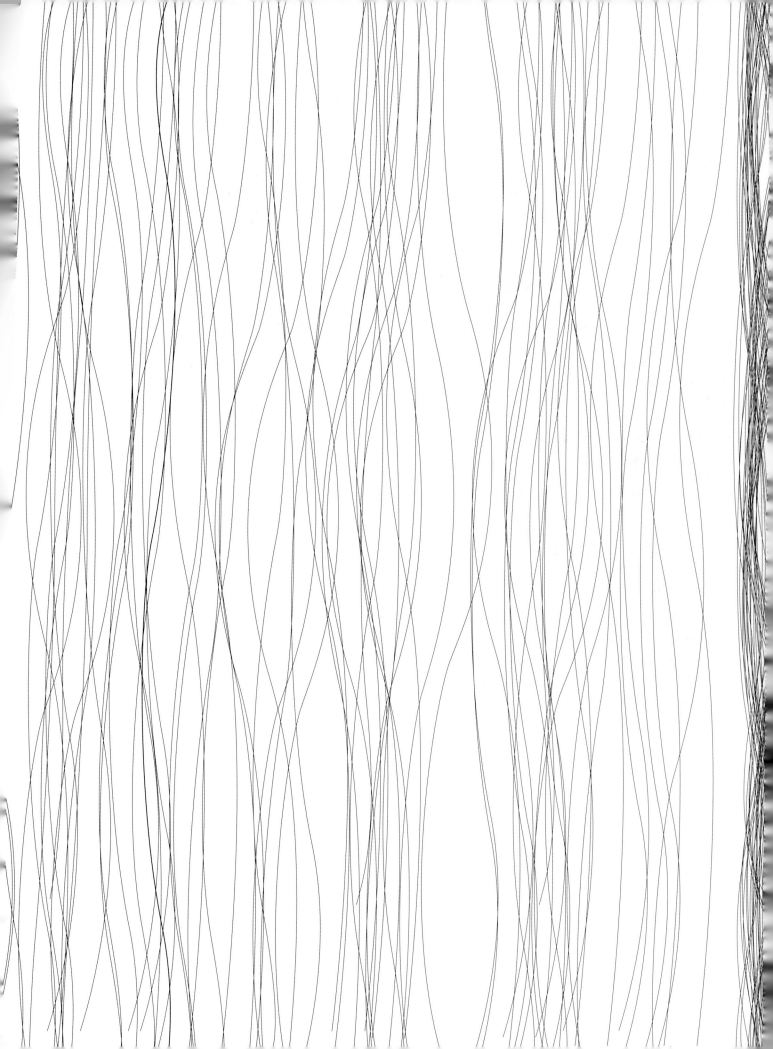

Aga Khan Award for Architecture
Retrospective 1977 – 2007

Over the past 30 years, the Aga Khan Award has recognised outstanding architectural achievements in some 32 countries. It has held seminars, conferences and exhibitions to explore and discuss the crucial issues of the built environment, and published the proceedings to bring these subjects to a wider audience. It has brought together the architectural community and policy-makers to celebrate the prize-winning projects of 10 award cycles in important historical and architectural settings, and has invited the leading thinkers and practitioners of the day to frame the discourse on architectural excellence within the context of successive master juries and steering committees.

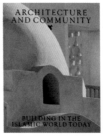
1st Cycle Award Ceremony Pakistan 1980

6th Cycle Award Ceremony Indonesia 1995

2nd Cycle Award Ceremony Turkey 1983

7th Cycle Award Ceremony Spain 1998

3rd Cycle Award Ceremony Morocco 1986

8th Cycle Award Ceremony Syria 2001

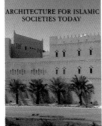
4th Cycle Award Ceremony Egypt 1989

9th Cycle Award Ceremony India 2004

5th Cycle Award Ceremony Uzbekistan 1992

10th Cycle Award Ceremony Malaysia 2007

18

ASIA

Landscaping Integration of the Soekarno-Hatta Airport
Indonesia 1992 Award

Kampung Kali Cho-de
Indonesia 1992 Award

Citra Niaga Urban Development
Indonesia 1989 Award

Kampung Kebalen Improvement
Indonesia 1986 Award

Saïd Naum Mosque
Indonesia 1986 Award

Pondok Pesantren Pabelan
Indonesia 1980 Award

Kampung Improvement Programme
Indonesia 1980 Award

Moulmein Rise Residential Tower
Singapore 2007 Award

University of Technology Petronas
Malaysia 2007 Award

Petronas Towers
Malaysia 2004 Award

Datai Hotel
Malaysia 2001 Award

Salinger Residence
Malaysia 1998 Award

Menara Mesiniaga
Malaysia 1992 Award

Tanjong Jara Beach Hotel and
Rantau Abang Visitors' Centre
Malaysia 1983 Award

Grameen Bank Housing Programme
Bangladesh 1989 Award

School in Rudrapur
Bangladesh 2007 Award

National Assembly Building,
Sher-e-Bangla Nagar
Bangladesh 1989 Award

Vidhan Bhavan
India 1998 Award

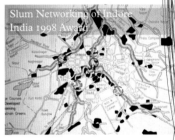
Slum Networking of Indore
India 1998 Award

Lepers Hospital
India 1998 Award

Aranya Community Housing
India 1992 Award

Entrepreneurship
Development Institute of India
India 1992 Award

Mughal Sheraton Hotel
India 1980 Award

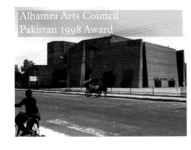
Alhamra Arts Council
Pakistan 1998 Award

Khuda-ki-Basti Incremental
Development Scheme
Pakistan 1992 Award

Bhong Mosque
Pakistan 1986 Award

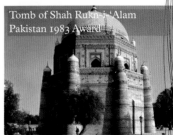
Tomb of Shah Rukn-i-'Alam
Pakistan 1983 Award

Restoration of Bukhara Old City
Uzbekistan 1992 Award

Bagh-e-Ferdowsi
Iran 2001 Award

New Life for Old Structures
Iran 2001 Award

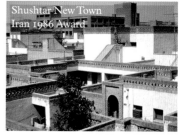
Shushtar New Town
Iran 1986 Award

Ali Qapu, Chehel Sutun and Hasht
Behesht, Iran 1980 Award

Stone Building System
Syria 1992 Award

Azem Palace
Syria 1983 Award

Samir Kassir Square
Lebanon 2007 Award

Great Omari Mosque
Lebanon 1989 Award

Old City of Jerusalem
Revitalisation Programme
Jerusalem 2004 Award

Al-Aqsa Mosque
Jerusalem 1986 Award

Rehabilitation of Hebron Old Town
Palestine 1998 Award

SOS Children's Village
Jordan 2001 Award

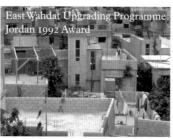
East Wahdat Upgrading Programme
Jordan 1992 Award

National Museum
Qatar 1980 Award

Water Towers
Kuwait 1980 Award

Tuwaiq Palace Saudi
Arabia 1998 Award

Great Mosque and Redevelopment
of the Old City Centre
Saudi Arabia 1992 Award

Al-Kindi Plaza
Saudi Arabia 1989 Award

Hayy Assafarat Landscaping
Saudi Arabia 1989 Award

Ministry of Foreign Affairs
Saudi Arabia 1989 Award

Inter-Continental Hotel and
Conference Centre
Saudi Arabia 1980 Award

Corniche Mosque
Saudi Arabia 1989 Award

Haj Terminal, King Abdul Aziz
International Airport
Saudi Arabia 1983 Award

Rehabilitation of the City of Shibam
Yemen 2007 Award

Restoration of the Amiriya Complex
Yemen 2007 Award

Restoration of Al-Abbas Mosque
Yemen 2004 Award

Conservation of Old Sana'a
Yemen 1992 Award

Aga Khan Award for Architecture, Retrospective 1977 – 2007

AFRICA

Bibliotheca Alexandrina
Egypt 2004 Award

Ismaïlliya Development Projects
Egypt 1986 Award

Nubian Museum
Egypt 2001 Award

Cultural Park for Children
Egypt 1992 Award

Ramses Wissa Wassef Arts Centre
Egypt 1983 Award

Darb Qirmiz Quarter
Egypt 1983 Award

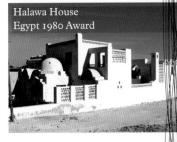

Halawa House
Egypt 1980 Award

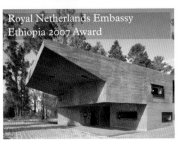

Royal Netherlands Embassy
Ethiopia 2007 Award

Panafrican Institute of Development
Burkina Faso 1992 Award

Primary School
Burkina Faso 2004 Award

Central Market
Burkina Faso 2007 Award

Kahere Eila Poultry Farming School
Guinea 2001 Award

Medical Centre
Mali 1980 Award

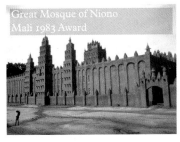

Great Mosque of Niono
Mali 1983 Award

Yaama Mosque
Niger 1986 Award

Agricultural Training Centre
Senegal 1980 Award

Alliance Franco-Sénégalaise
Senegal 1992 Award

Kaedi Regional Hospital
Mauritania 1992 Award

Courtyard Houses
Morocco 1980 Award

Dar Lamane Housing
Morocco 1986 Award

Rehabilitation of Asilah
Morocco 1989 Award

Aït Iktel
Morocco 2001 Award

Sidi Bou Saïd
Tunisia 1980 Award

Hafsia Quarter I
Tunisia 1983 Award

MAQUETTE HAFSIA

Résidence Andalous
Tunisia 1983 Award

Sidi el-Aloui Primary School
Tunisia 1989 Award

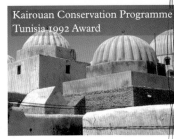

Kairouan Conservation Programme
Tunisia 1992 Award

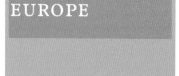
Hafsia Quarter II
Tunisia 1992 Award

EUROPE

Institut du Monde Arabe
France 1989 Award

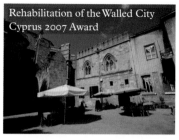
Rehabilitation of the Walled City
Cyprus 2007 Award

Sherefudin's White Mosque
Bosnia-Herzegovina 1983 Award

Mostar Old Town
Bosnia-Herzegovina 1986 Award

Turkish Historical Society
Turkey 1980 Award

Rüstem Pasha Caravenserai
Turkey 1980 Award

Ertegün House
Turkey 1980 Award

Nail Çakirhan House
Turkey 1983 Award

Social Security Complex
Turkey 1986 Award

Historic Sites Development
Turkey 1986 Award

Gürel Family Summer Residence
Turkey 1989 Award

Palace Parks Programme
Turkey 1992 Award

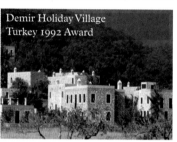
Demir Holiday Village
Turkey 1992 Award

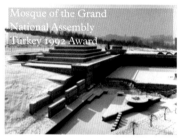
Mosque of the Grand
National Assembly
Turkey 1992 Award

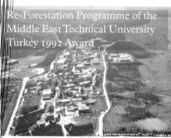
Re-Forestation Programme of the
Middle East Technical University
Turkey 1992 Award

Olbia Social Centre
Turkey 2001 Award

B2 House
Turkey 2004 Award

Sandbag Shelter Prototypes
Various Locations Worldwide
2004 Award

CHAIRMAN'S
AWARDS

Hassan Fathy 1980

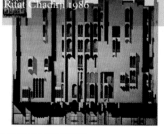
Rifat Chadirji 1986

Geoffrey Bawa, 2001

SEMINARS

Toward an
Architecture
in the Spirit
of Islam
France 1978

Conservation
as Cultural
Survival
Turkey 1978

Housing:
Process and
Physical Form
Indonesia 1979

186

Architecture as Symbol and Self-Identity Morocco 1979

Places of Public Gathering in Islam Jordan 1980

The Changing Rural Habitat China 1981

The Changing Rural Habitat China 1981

The Changing Rural Habitat China 1981

The Changing Rural Habitat China 1981

The Changing Rural Habitat China 1981

The Changing Rural Habitat China 1981

Reading the Contemporary African City Senegal 1982

Reading the Contemporary African City Senegal 1982

Architecture and Identity Malaysia 1983

Development and Urban Metamorphosis, Yemen at the Cross-Roads Yemen 1983

Development and Urban Metamorphosis, Yemen at the Cross-Roads Yemen 1983

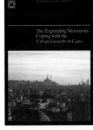
The Expanding Metropolis: Coping with the Urban Growth of Cairo Egypt 1984

The Expanding Metropolis: Coping with the Urban Growth of Cairo Egypt 1984

Regionalism in Architecture Bangladesh 1985

Architecture Education in the Islamic World Spain 1986

Criticism in Architecture Malta 1987

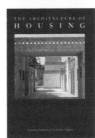
The Architecture of Housing Zanzibar 1988

Expressions of Islam in Buildings Indonesia 1990

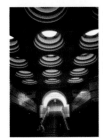
The Built Environment of Central Asia Today Kazakhstan 1996

Shelter: The Access To Hope Turkey 1996

Contemporary Architecture in the Middle East Jordan 1997

The New Architecture of the Caucas and Central Asia Azerbaijan 1999

Architecture Re-introduced, New Projects in Societies in Change Lebanon 1999

Expression of Faith in Contemporary Architecture Russia 2000

Architecture for a Changing World Iran 2002

Architectural Critisims and Journalism Kuwait 2005

Doğan Tekeli · Elías Torres Tur · Billie Tsien · Han Tümertekin · Jafar Tukan · Mahbub Ul-Haq · Robert Venturi · Parid Wardi bin Sudin · Kenneth Yeang · Saïd Zulficar

Members of On Site Review Team

Galal Abada · Abdelhalim I. Abdelhalim · Jellal Abdelkafi · Samir Abdulac · Arya Abieta · Akram Abu Hamdan · Farokh Afshar · Jamel Akbar · Hana Alamuddin · Mohammad Al-Asad · Mokhless Al-Hirari · Sahel Al-Hiyari · Zainab Faruqui Ali · Mashary Al-Naim · Selma Al-Radi · Abbad Al-Radi · Wael Al-Samhouri · Nur Altinyildiz · Khaled Asfour · Shukur Askarov · Isam Awwad · Aydan Balamir · Naima Chabbi-Chemrouk · Yekta Chahrouzi · William Curtis · Salma Samar Damluji · Darab Diba · Lailun Ekram · Dalila ElKerdany · Homeyra Ettehadieh · Rawia Fadel · Nasrine Faghih · Reha Günay · Abdul Majid Hajeedar · Omar Hallaj · Tanvir Hasan · Arif Hasan · Mukhtar Husain · Abuhamdan Imamuddin · Syed Zaigham Jaffery · Khadija Jamal-Shaban · Hanif Kara · Romi Khosla · Jolyon Leslie · Ronald Lewcock · Jimmy Lim · Rahul Mehrotra · Lazlo Mester de Parajd · Ralph Mills-Tettey · Saïd Mouline · Abdul Wassay Najimi · John Norton · Darl Rastorfer · Piers Rodgers · Ildar Sabitov · Kamran Safamensh · Ashraf Salama · Serge Santelli · John Silas · Raoul Snelder · Michael Sorkin · Fredj Stambouli · Budi Sukada · Brian Brace Taylor · Nader Tehrani · Gunawan Tjahjono · Okan Üstünkök · Fernando Varanda · Dorothée Vauzelles · Archibald Walls · Ayşil Yavuz · Yildirim Yavuz · Kenneth Yeang · Atilla Yücel

Award Secretariat

Farrokh Derakhshani · Renata Holod · Jack Kennedy · Hasan-Uddin Khan · Suha Özkan · Saïd Zulficar

2007 Award Steering Committee and Master Jury

Seated, left to right
Shirazeh Houshiary, Kenneth Yeang, Prince Hussain Aga Khan, His Highness the Aga Khan, Princess Khaliya Aga Khan, Brigitte Shim, Rashid Khalidi

Standing, first row, left to right
Mohsen Mostafavi, Modjtaba Sadria, Homa Farjadi, Han Tümertekin, Omar Akbar, Glenn Lowry, Farshid Moussavi

Standing, second row, left to right
Hani Rashid, Homi Bhabha, Okwui Enwezor, Sahel Al-Hiyari, Billie Tsien, Farrokh Derakhshani

2007 Steering Committee

His Highness the Aga Khan
Chairman

Omar Akbar
Urbanist and architect; Executive Director, Bauhaus Dessau Foundation, Dessau, Germany

Jacques Herzog
Architect; Partner, Herzog & de Meuron Architects, Basel, Switzerland

Glenn Lowry
Art historian; Director, Museum of Modern Art, New York, USA

Mohsen Mostafavi
Architect and professor; Dean, College of Architecture, Art, and Planning, Cornell University, Ithaca, USA

Farshid Moussavi
Architect; Partner, Foreign Office Architects, London, and Professor in Practice of Architecture, Harvard University, USA

Hani Rashid
Architect; Partner, Asymptote Architecture, New York, and Professor of Architecture at Columbia University, New York and the Swiss Federal Institute of Technology, Zurich, Switzerland

Modjtaba Sadria
Philosopher; Professor at Institute for the Study of Muslim Civilisations-AKU, London, UK

Billie Tsien
Architect and artist; Partner, Tod Williams Billie Tsien Architects, New York, USA

Farrokh Derakhshani
Director, Aga Khan Award for Architecture

2007 Master Jury

Sahel Al-Hiyari
Architect and painter; Principal, Sahel Al-Hiyari
and Partners, Jordan

Homi K. Bhabha
Cultural theoretician; Anne F. Rothenberg
Professor of the Humanities, Department of
English, and Director of the Humanities Center,
Harvard University, USA

Okwui Enwezor
Curator, critic, and poet; Dean of Academic
Affairs and Senior Vice President, San Francisco
Art Institute, USA

Homa Farjadi
Architect; Principal, Farjadi Architects, UK, and
Professor in Practice of Architecture, University of
Pennsylvania, USA

Shirazeh Houshiary
Artist, UK

Rashid Khalidi
Historian; Edward Said Professor of Arab Studies,
History Department, and Director of the Middle
East Institute, Columbia University, New York, USA

Brigitte Shim
Architect; Partner, Shim-Sutcliffe Architects, and
Professor of Architecture, Landscape, and Design,
University of Toronto, Canada

Han Tümertekin
Architect; Principal, Mimarlar Tasarim ve
Danismanlik, Turkey

Kenneth Yeang
Architect-Planner; Principal, Llewelyn Davies
Yeang, UK, and Hamzah & Yeang, Malaysia